BOOK OF MORMON CHIASMUS

BOOK OF MORMON CHIASMUS

292 Extraordinary Examples

Donald W. Parry

STONEWELL PRESS

ISBN 978-1-62730-123-7

Stonewell Press
Salt Lake City, UT
stonewellpress.com

Typography: Jack M. Lyon, The Editorium
Cover design: Nathaniel J. Parry

Contents

Introduction   7

1 Nephi   13
2 Nephi   34
Jacob   46
Enos, Omni, and Words of Mormon   49
Mosiah   52
Alma   66
Helaman   103
3 Nephi   118
4 Nephi and Mormon   131
Ether   134
Moroni   140

Appendix   143
Selected Bibliography   150

Introduction

Chiasmus is an inverted parallelism or a series of mirrored lines; it is a presentation of a series of ideas or words followed by a second presentation of similar words or ideas, but in reverse order.[1] Chiasmus has been defined as "a rhetorical or literary figure in which words, grammatical constructions, or concepts are repeated in reverse order, in the same or a modified form."[2]

The Old Testament presents hundreds of chiasms of various sizes;[3] the book of Isaiah alone has more than one hundred.[4] Chiasmus can vary in size—from four lines to entire chapters (see, for example, 1 Kings 17–19).

Three examples of a simple chiasmus are found in Isaiah 5:20:

A Woe unto them that call **evil**
   B **good**,
   B and **good**
A **evil**;
A that put **darkness**
   B for **light**,
   B and **light**
A for **darkness**;

---

[1] Welch, "Chiasm, Chiasmus: I. Ancient Near East and Hebrew Bible/Old Testament," 5:78. For an important examination of chiasmus in the ancient world, examine Welch, *Chiasmus in Antiquity.* For the significance of chiasmus, consult Welch, "What Does Chiasmus in the Book of Mormon Prove?" 199–224.

[2] Dictionary 2.2.2 (203) Copyright 2005–2017 Apple Inc.

[3] Chiasms are of varying sizes and lengths. Elder Jeffrey R. Holland, for example, set forth a chiasmus that spans several chapters in 2 Nephi (from 3 Nephi 11:8–18:39) in *Christ and the New Covenant,* 275.

[4] For a list of chiastic structures found in the book of Isaiah, including key words and scriptural references, see Appendix.

A that put **bitter**
  B for **sweet**,
  B and **sweet**
A for **bitter**!

Here the terms *evil* and *good* are presented once and then again in reverse order. The verse also includes two other simple chiasms: *darkness/light/light/darkness* followed by *bitter/sweet/sweet/bitter*.

Another example is Isaiah 6:10:

A Make the **heart** of this people fat,
  B and make their **ears** heavy,
    C and shut their **eyes**;
    C lest they see with their **eyes**,
  B and hear with their **ears**,
A and understand with their **heart**.

In this verse, the words *heart*, *ears*, and *eyes* are presented and then are repeated in reverse order, a simple chiasm.

Isaiah 60:1–3 presents a longer chiastic structure, with an ABCDEFG//GFEDCBA pattern:

A **Arise**,
  B shine;
    C for thy **light** is come,
      D and the **glory**
        E of the **Lord**
          F is risen upon thee.
            G For, behold, the **darkness** shall cover the earth,
            G and gross **darkness** the people:
          F but shall **arise** upon thee,
        E the **Lord**
      D and his **glory** shall be seen upon thee,
    C and the nations shall come to thy **light**
  B and kings to the **brightness**
A of thy **rising** (Isa. 60:1–3) [translation by the author]

One additional example from the Bible, which pertains to the Elijah Narrative, covers three chapters in 1 Kings (1 Kgs. 17–19):

A The Lord directs Elijah to go to Transjordan (17:2–7)

   B Elijah travels north of Israel (17:8–24)

   C Elijah returns to Israel (18:1–2)

   D Obadiah and Ahab travel (18:3–6)

   E Dialogue of Elijah and Obadiah (18:7–15)

   F Meeting of Elijah and Ahab (18:16–20)

   G Baal's prophets are not successful in calling down fire (18:21–29)

   G Elijah successfully calls down fire (18:30–40)

   F Meeting of Elijah and Ahab (18:41–42)

   E Dialogue of Elijah and his servant (18:43–45)

   D Ahab and Elijah travel to Jezreel (18:45–46)

   C Elijah flees Israel (19:1–3)

   B Elijah travels south of Israel (19:3–18)

A The Lord directs Elijah to go to Transjordan (1 Kgs. 19:19–21)

The Book of Mormon contains more than three hundred[5] instances of chiasmus;[6] each one is unique, impactful, and inspiring. This is a remarkable number. The following examples from the Book of Mormon are formatted to make them more readable and pleasing to the eye. (These are adapted from Parry, *Poetic Parallelisms in the Book of Mormon*, Stonewell Press, 2019.) Key expressions are underlined to highlight the parallels.

---

[5] For the number three hundred and the actual Book of Mormon examples, consult Parry, *Poetic Parallelisms in the Book of Mormon*, passim. For a list of chiasms in the Book of Mormon, see the Index of Poetic Forms, ibid., 565. Note also my forthcoming paper that deals with chiasmus in the Hebrew Bible (specifically the Leningrad Codex) versus the Dead Sea Scrolls texts of Isaiah, "Chiasmus in the Text of Isaiah: MT Isaiah Versus the Great Isaiah Scroll (1QIsaa)," in Welch and Parry, *Chiasmus: The State of the Art*.

[6] As a young missionary, John W. Welch discovered examples of chiasmus in the Book of Mormon; subsequently, over the decades, he has published a number of important articles on the topic, including: "Chiasm, Chiasmus: I. Ancient Near East and Hebrew Bible/Old Testament," 5:78–79; "Chiasmus in the Book of Mormon." In *Book of Mormon Authorship*, 33–52; "Chiasmus in the Book of Mormon," *BYU Studies Quarterly*, 69–83; "Chiasmus in the Book of Mormon," *New Era*, 6–11; "Criteria for Identifying and Evaluating the Presence of Chiasmus," *Journal of Book of Mormon Studies*, 1–14; and "A Masterpiece: Alma 36," *Rediscovering the Book of Mormon*, 114–131. For a study of chiasmus in Mesoamerican texts, examine the publication of Christenson, "Chiasmus in Mesoamerican Texts," 233–35.

Second Nephi 9:20 is a beautifully simple chiasmus about God's omniscience:

A For he **knoweth**
  B **all things**,
  B and there is **not anything**
A save he **knows** it. (2 Ne. 9:20)

While this example is very brief, it contains clear-cut boundaries, is nicely balanced, and delivers a forceful testimony about the knowledge of God.

In only a few lines, Alma 34:10 features a chiasmus that presents essential truth about Jesus's infinite and eternal sacrifice:

A there should be a **great and last sacrifice**;
  B yea, not a **sacrifice of man**,
    C neither of **beast**,
    C neither of any manner of **fowl**;
  B for it shall not be a **human sacrifice**;
A but it must be an **infinite and eternal sacrifice**. (Alma 34:10)

Mosiah 3:18–19 gives us a chiasmus that focuses on Jesus Christ and his atoning blood.

A they **humble** themselves
  B and become as little **children**,
    C and believe that salvation was, and is, and is to come, in and through the **atoning blood of Christ**, the Lord Omnipotent.
      D For the **natural man**
        E is an enemy to **God**,
          F and **has been** from the fall of Adam,
          F and **will be**, forever and ever,
        E unless he yields to the enticings of the **Holy Spirit**,
      D and putteth off the **natural man**
    C and becometh a saint through the **atonement of Christ** the Lord,
  B and becometh as a **child**,
A submissive, meek, **humble** . . . (Mosiah 3:18–19)

Jesus Christ is clearly the focus of this passage, as can be seen by the use of the key expressions *atoning blood of Christ, Lord Omnipotent, God,* and *atonement of Christ the Lord.* This passage also gives prominence to six primary mirrored words and phrases: *humble/humble, children/child, atoning blood of Christ/atonement of Christ, natural man/natural man,* and *God/Holy Spirit.* As with all chiastic passages, the message of these verses is greater than the creative arrangement of the words. But both together—the message and the presentation—produce a powerful communication to the reader.

Another example of a chiastic passage is found in Mosiah 2:

A And it came to pass that when they came up to the **temple,**

  B they **pitched their tents** round about,

    C every man according to his **family,**

      D consisting of his wife, and his **sons,** and his **daughters,**

      D and their **sons,** and their **daughters,** from the eldest down to the youngest,

    C every **family** being separate one from another.

  B And they **pitched their tents**

A round about the **temple** (Mosiah 2:5–6)

On the surface, this chiasmus may not seem very profound. But it actually teaches an important truth about family togetherness—and about families centering themselves in the temple.

Miscellaneous Notes

1. The Book of Mormon examples of chiasmus in this book have been formatted to make them more readable and pleasing to the eye. Key expressions are in bold to highlight parallel lines and corresponding elements.

2. For the purposes of this book, every example of chiasmus has been extracted, sometimes abruptly, from its context in the Book of Mormon. To better and fully appreciate each chiasmus, one must go back to the Book of Mormon and read it in its greater frame of reference.

3. Not every example of chiasmus has the same degree of chiasticity, meaning, some examples of chiasmus are of a higher quality than others. Of course, seeking higher quality examples of chiasmus is a relative matter—one individual's favorite chiasmus may be different from another's; everyone may have their own most-liked chiasmus.

4. The 292 examples of chiasmus in this volume belong solely to the Book of Mormon prophets and writers. Although the Isaiah chapters that are cited in the Book of Mormon contain many examples of chiasmus, they are not listed in this volume. For examples of many chiasms in Isaiah, see the appendix to this book.

5. The 292 chiasms in this volume are representative examples. They do not constitute a comprehensive listing of all chiasms in the Book of Mormon.

6. Finally, it is noteworthy that John W. Welch, Brigham Young University law professor (emeritus), founder of the Foundation for Ancient Research and Mormon Studies, and cofounder and chairman of Book of Mormon Central, has recently launched Chiasmus International. That project will be using *Book of Mormon Chiasmus: 292 Extraordinary Examples* as one of its featured sources, as numerous chiastic structures will be presented and analyzed in a wide variety of languages, including Albanian, Chinese, French, German, Hawaiian, Japanese, Polish, Russian, Serbian, Swedish, and many others. This grand comparative literary effort will be available at chiasmusresources.org and bookofmormoncentral.org. This multilingual array will no doubt enhance the world's appreciation for the Book of Mormon in many insightful and inspiring ways.

1 Nephi

1 NEPHI 1:1–3—
NEPHI MAKES HIS RECORD

A yea, having had a great **knowledge** of the goodness and the mysteries of God,

    B therefore I make a **record** of my proceedings in my days. (1:1)

        C Yea, I make a record in the **language** of my father,

            D which consists of the **learning of the Jews**

        C and the **language** of the Egyptians. (1:2)

    B And I know that the **record** which I make is true: and I make it with mine own hand:

A and I make it according to my **knowledge**. (1:3)

1 NEPHI 1:16—

NEPHI SPEAKS OF LEHI'S RECORD
BUT GIVES AN ABRIDGED ACCOUNT

A And now I, Nephi, do **not make a full account**

    B of the things which my **father hath written**,

        C for he hath **written many things**

            D which he saw in **visions**

            D and in **dreams**;

        C and he also hath **written many things**

    B which **he prophesied and spake** unto his children,

A of which I shall **not make a full account**. (1:16)

1 NEPHI 1:17—
NEPHI ABRIDGES LEHI'S RECORD

A But I shall make an **account of my proceedings in my days**.
  B Behold, I make an **abridgment of the record** of my father,
    C Upon plates which **I have made**
    C with **mine own hands**;
  B wherefore, after I have **abridged the record** of my father
A then will I make an **account of mine own life**. (1:17)

1 NEPHI 1:18—
LEHI PROPHESIES

A that after **the Lord had shown**
  B so many marvelous **things** unto my father, Lehi, yea, concerning the destruction of Jerusalem,
    C behold he went forth among the **people**,
      D and began **to prophesy**
      D and **to declare**
    C unto **them**
  B concerning the **things**
A which **he had both seen** and heard. (1:18)

1 NEPHI 1:20–2:1—
THE WICKED SEEK LEHI'S LIFE

A and they also **sought** his **life**, that they might **take it away**.
  B But behold, I, Nephi, will show unto you that the tender mercies of the Lord are over all those whom he hath chosen, **because of their faith**, to make them mighty even unto the power of deliverance. (1:20)
    C For behold, it came to pass that the Lord **spake unto my father**, yea, even in a dream,
    C and **said unto him**: Blessed art thou Lehi, because of the things which thou hast done;
  B and **because thou hast been faithful** and declared unto this people the things which I commanded thee,
A behold, they **seek to take away thy life**. (2:1)

1 Nephi 2:2–4—
Lehi Is Obedient to the Lord

A and **depart into the wilderness**. (2:2)
  B And **it came to pass** that
    C **he was obedient** unto the word of the **Lord**,
    C wherefore **he did** as the **Lord commanded him**. (2:3)
  B And **it came to pass** that
A he **departed into the wilderness**. (2:4)

1 Nephi 2:4–5—
Lehi and His Family Travel in the Wilderness

A save it were **his family**,
  B and provisions, and tents, and departed **into the wilderness**. (2:4)
    C And he came down by the **borders** near the shore of the **Red Sea**;
      D and he traveled **in the wilderness**
    C in the **borders** which are nearer the **Red Sea**;
  B and he did travel **in the wilderness**
A with **his family**, (2:5)

1 Nephi 3:3–12—
Nephi and His Brothers Seek the Brass Plates

A For behold, **Laban** hath the **record** of the Jews and also a **genealogy of my forefathers**, and they are **engraven upon plates of brass**. (3:3)
  B Wherefore, the Lord hath commanded me that thou and thy brothers should go unto the **house of Laban**, and seek the records, and bring them down hither into the wilderness. (3:4)
    C And now, behold thy **brothers** murmur saying it is a hard thing which I have required of them; but behold I have not required it of them, but it is a commandment of the Lord. (3:5)
      D Therefore go, my son, and thou shalt be favored of the Lord, because thou hast not murmured. (3:6) And it came to pass that **I, Nephi**,
        E said unto **my father**:
          F I will go and **do the things** which

> **G** the **Lord** hath **commanded**, for I know that
> **G** the **Lord** giveth no **commandments** unto the
> children of men,
>> **F** save he shall prepare a way for them that they may
>> **accomplish the thing** which he commandeth them.
>> (3:7)
>>> **E** And it came to pass that when **my father** had heard
>>> these words he was exceedingly glad for he knew that I had
>>> been blessed of the Lord. (3:8)
>>>> **D** And **I, Nephi**, and my brethren took our journey in the
>>>> wilderness, with our tents, to go up to the land of Jerusalem.
>>>> (3:9)
>>> **C** And it came to pass that when we had gone up to the land of
>>> Jerusalem, I and my **brethren** did consult one with another.
>>> (3:10)
>> **B** And we cast lots—who of us should go in unto the **house of
>> Laban**. And it came to pass that the lot fell upon Laman; and Laman
>> went in unto the **house of Laban**, and he talked with him as he sat
>> in his house. (3:11)
> **A** And he desired of **Laban** the **records** which were **engraven upon
> the plates of brass**, which contained the **genealogy of my father**.
> (3:12)

1 Nephi 3:16–22—
The Importance of the Brass Plates

> **A** therefore let us go **down to the land** of our father's **inheritance**, for
> behold he left **gold** and **silver**, and all manner of **riches**. (3:16)
>> **B** And all this he hath done because of the **commandments of the
>> Lord.** For he knew that Jerusalem must be destroyed, because of the
>> wickedness of the people. (3:17)
>>> **C** For behold, they have rejected the **words of the prophets**.
>>> Wherefore if my father should dwell in the land after he hath been
>>> commanded to flee out of the land, behold, he would also perish.
>>> Wherefore, it must needs be that he flee out of the land. (3:18)
>>>> **D** And behold, it is wisdom in God that we should obtain
>>>> these records, **that we may preserve** unto our children the
>>>> **language** of our fathers; (3:19)

D And also **that we may preserve** unto them the **words** which have been

C spoken by the **mouth of all the holy prophets**, which have been delivered unto them by the Spirit and power of God, since the world began, even down unto this present time. (3:20)

B And it came to pass that after this manner of language did I persuade my brethren, that they be faithful in keeping the **commandments of God**. (3:21)

A And it came to pass that we went **down to the land** of our **inheritance**, and we did gather together our **gold**, and our **silver**, and our **precious things**. (3:22)

1 NEPHI 4:5–24—
NEPHI IS LED BY THE SPIRIT AND FINDS LABAN

A And it was by night; and I caused that they should hide themselves **without the walls**.

B And after they had hid themselves, I, Nephi, crept into the city and went forth towards the **house of Laban**. (4:5) And I was led by the Spirit, not knowing beforehand the things which I should do. (4:6) Nevertheless I went forth, and as I came near unto the **house of Laban** I beheld a man, and he had fallen to the earth before me, for he was drunken with wine. (4:7) And when I came to him I found that **it was Laban**. (4:8)

C And I beheld his **sword**, and I drew it forth from the sheath thereof; and the hilt thereof was of pure gold, and the workman-ship thereof was exceedingly fine, and I saw that the blade thereof was of the most precious steel. (4:9)

D And it came to pass that I was constrained by the **Spirit** that I should kill Laban; but I said in my heart: Never at any time have I shed the blood of man. And I shrunk and would that I might not slay him. (4:10) And the **Spirit** said unto me again: Behold the Lord hath delivered him into thy hands. Yea, and I also knew that he had sought to take away mine own life; yea, and he would not hearken unto the command-ments of the Lord; and he also had taken away our property. (4:11)

E And it came to pass that the Spirit said unto me again: Slay him, for **the Lord hath delivered** him into thy hands; (4:12) Behold the Lord slayeth the wicked to bring forth his righteous purposes. It is better that one man should perish than that a nation should dwindle and perish in unbelief. (4:13)

> **F** And now, when I, Nephi, had heard these words, I remembered the words of the Lord which he spake unto me in the wilderness, saying that: Inasmuch as thy seed shall **keep my commandments**, they shall prosper in the land of promise. (4:14)
>
> **F** Yea, and I also thought that they could not **keep the commandments** of the Lord according to the law of Moses, save they should have the law. (4:15) And I also knew that the law was engraven upon the plates of brass. (4:16)

E And again, I knew that **the Lord had delivered** Laban into my hands for this cause—that I might obtain the records according to his commandments. (4:17)

D Therefore I did obey the voice of the **Spirit**, and took Laban by the hair of the head, and I smote off his head with his own sword. (4:18)

C And after I had smitten off his head with his own **sword**, I took the garments of Laban and put them upon mine own body; yea, even every whit; and I did gird on his armor about my loins. (4:19)

B And after I had done this, I went forth unto the **treasury of Laban**. And as I went forth towards the **treasury of Laban**, behold, I saw the **servant of Laban** who had the keys of the treasury. And I commanded him in the voice of Laban, that he should go with me into the treasury. (4:20) And he supposed me to be his master, Laban, for he beheld the garments and also the sword girded about my loins. (4:21) And he spake unto me concerning the elders of the Jews, he knowing that his master, Laban, had been out by night among them. (4:22) And I spake unto him as if it had been Laban. (4:23)

A And I also spake unto him that I should carry the engravings, which were upon the plates of brass, to my elder brethren, who were **without the walls**. (4:24)

1 Nephi 4:32—
"As the Lord Liveth"

A that if he would hearken unto my **words**,

 B as the Lord **liveth**,

 B and as I **live**,

A even so **that if he would hearken** unto our **words**, we would spare his **life**.

1 Nephi 4:33–35—
Nephi Speaks to Zoram with an Oath

A And **I spake** unto him, even with an oath,

 B that he need **not fear**;

  C that he should be a **free man like unto us**

   D if he would **go down in the wilderness** with us. (4:33)

    E And I also spake unto him, saying: Surely the **Lord** hath **commanded**

     F us to **do this thing**;

     F and shall **we** not **be diligent**

    E in keeping the **commandments** of the **Lord**?

   D Therefore, if thou wilt **go down into the wilderness** to my father

  C thou shalt **have place with us**. (4:34)

 B And it came to pass that Zoram did **take courage**

A at the words which **I spake**. (4:35)

1 Nephi 4:38–5:6—
Lehi Is a Visionary Man

A And it came to pass that we took the **plates of brass** and the servant of Laban,

 B and departed into **the wilderness**,

  C and **journeyed** unto the tent of our father. (4:38)

   D And it came to pass that after we had come down into the wilderness unto **our father**, behold, he was filled with joy, and also **my mother**, **Sariah**, was exceedingly glad, for she truly had mourned because of us. (5:1)

E For she had supposed that we **had perished** in the wilderness;

    F and she also had **complained against my father**, telling him that he was a **visionary man**; saying:

        G Behold thou hast led us forth from the land of our inheritance, and **my sons are no more**,

        G and **we perish in the wilderness**. (5:2)

    F And after this manner of language had my mother **complained against my father**. (5:3) And it had come to pass that my father spake unto her, saying: I know that I am a **visionary man**; for if I had not seen the things of God in a vision I should not have known the goodness of God,

E but had tarried at Jerusalem, and **had perished** with my brethren. (5:4) But behold, I have obtained a land of promise, in the which things I do rejoice; yea, and I know that the Lord will deliver my sons out of the hands of Laban, and bring them down again unto us in the wilderness. (5:5)

  D And after this manner of language did **my father**, Lehi, comfort **my mother**, **Sariah**,

 C concerning us, while we **journeyed**

B in **the wilderness** up to the land of Jerusalem

A to obtain the **record of the Jews**. (5:6)

1 NEPHI 5:7–9—
SARIAH HAS A SURE WITNESS

A behold **their joy was full**, and my mother was comforted. (5:7)

 B And **she spake**, saying:

  C Now I know of a surety that **the Lord hath commanded** my husband to flee into the wilderness;

    D yea, and I also know of a surety that the Lord hath **protected my sons**,

    D and **delivered them** out of the hands of Laban,

  C and given them power whereby they could accomplish the thing which **the Lord hath commanded** them.

 B And after this manner of language did **she speak**. (5:8)

A And it came to pass that **they did rejoice exceedingly**, (5:9)

1 Nephi 5:14–16—
Lehi Discovers that He Is a Descendant of Joseph

A And it came to pass that **my father**, **Lehi**, also found upon the plates of brass a **genealogy of his fathers**; wherefore he knew that he was a **descendant of Joseph**; yea, even that Joseph who was the son of Jacob, who was sold into Egypt,

    B and who was preserved by the hand of the Lord, that he might **preserve** his **father**, **Jacob**, **and all his household** from perishing with famine. (5:14)

        C And they were also led **out of captivity**

        C and **out of** the land of **Egypt**,

    B by that same God who had **preserved them**. (5:15)

A And thus **my father**, **Lehi**, did discover the **genealogy of his fathers**. And Laban also was a **descendant of Joseph**, wherefore he and his fathers had kept the records. (5:16)

1 Nephi 5:17–20—
The Brass Plates Will Never Perish

A And now when **my father** saw all these things, he was filled with the Spirit,

    B and began to **prophesy concerning his seed**— (5:17)

        C That these **plates of brass** should go forth

           D unto **all nations, kindreds, tongues,**

           D and **people** who were of his seed. (5:18)

        C Wherefore, he said that these **plates of brass** should never perish; neither should they be dimmed any more by time.

    B And he **prophesied** many things **concerning his seed** (5:19)

A And it came to pass that thus far I and **my father** had kept the commandments wherewith the Lord had commanded us. (5:20)

1 Nephi 6:1–2—
Lehi and His Family Are Descendants of Joseph

A And now I, Nephi, do not give the **genealogy** of my father in this part of my record

    B **neither** at any time **shall I give it** after upon **these plates**

> **C** which **I am writing**;
>> **D** for it is given in the record
> **C** which has been **kept by my father**;
B wherefore, **I do not write it** in **this work**. (6:1)
A For it sufficeth me to say that we are **descendants** of Joseph. (6:2)

1 Nephi 7:3–5—
Ishmael and His Family Join Lehi's Family

A And it came to pass that I, Nephi, did again, with my brethren, go **forth into the wilderness**
> **B** **to go up** to Jerusalem. (7:3)
>> **C** And it came to pass that we went up unto the **house of Ishmael**,
>>> **D** and we did **gain favor** in the sight **of Ishmael**,
>>>> **E** insomuch that we did speak unto him the words of the Lord. (7:4)
>>> **D** And it came to pass that the Lord did **soften the heart of Ishmael**,
>> **C** and also **his household**,
> **B** insomuch that they **took their journey** with us
A **down into the wilderness** to the tent of our father. (7:5)

1 Nephi 7:13—
The Lord's Word Will Be Fulfilled

A the word of the Lord shall **be fulfilled**
> **B** concerning the **destruction of Jerusalem**;
>> **C** for all things which the Lord hath spoken
> **B** concerning the **destruction of Jerusalem**
A must **be fulfilled**.

1 Nephi 7:16–19—
Nephi's Brothers Are Angry with Him

And it came to pass that when I, Nephi, had spoken these words unto my brethren,

A **they were angry with me**. And it came to pass that **they did lay their hands upon me**, for behold, they were exceedingly wroth, and they did bind me with cords, for they sought **to take away my life**, that they might leave me in the wilderness to be devoured by wild beasts. (7:16)

> **B** But it came to pass that **I prayed** unto the Lord, saying:
>> **C** O Lord, according to my faith which is in thee, **wilt thou deliver me** from the hands of my brethren;
>> **C** yea, even give me strength **that I may burst these bands** with which I am bound. (7:17)
> **B** And it came to pass that when **I had said these words**, behold, the bands were loosed from off my hands and feet, and I stood before my brethren, and I spake unto them again. (7:18)

A And it came to pass that **they were angry with me** again, and sought to **lay hands upon me**; but behold, one of the daughters of Ishmael, yea, and also her mother, and one of the sons of Ishmael, did plead with my brethren, insomuch that they did soften their hearts; and they did cease striving **to take away my life**. (7:19)

1 NEPHI 8:8–9—
LEHI PRAYS FOR MERCY

And after I had traveled for the space of many hours in darkness,
> **A** I began to **pray unto the Lord**
>> **B** that he would have **mercy** on me,
>> **B** according to the multitude of his tender **mercies**. (8:8)
> **A** And it came to pass after I had **prayed unto the Lord** (8:9)

1 NEPHI 8:10–12—
LEHI PARTAKES OF THE FRUIT OF THE TREE OF LIFE

> **A** And it came to pass that I beheld a tree, whose fruit was **desirable**
>> **B** to make one **happy**. (8:10)
>>> **C** And it came to pass that **I** did go forth and **partake of the fruit thereof**;
>>>> **D** and I beheld that **it was most sweet, above all** that **I ever** before tasted.

D Yea, and I beheld that the **fruit thereof was white, to exceed all** the whiteness that **I had ever** seen. (8:11)

C And as **I partook of the fruit thereof**

B it filled my soul with exceedingly great **joy**;

A wherefore, I began to be **desirous** (8:12)

1 NEPHI 8:22–23—
THE "MIST OF DARKNESS" CAUSES SOME TO BECOME LOST

A And it came to pass that **they did come** forth,

B and **commence in the path** which led to the tree. (8:22)

C And it came to pass that there arose a **mist of darkness**;

C yea, even an exceedingly great **mist of darkness**,

B insomuch that they who had **commenced in the path** did lose their way,

A that **they wandered off** and were lost. (8:23)

1 NEPHI 11:32—
THE LAMB OF GOD

A And **I looked** and beheld

B the **Lamb of God**, that he was taken by the people;

B yea, the **Son of the everlasting God** was judged of the world;

A and **I saw** and bear record. (11:32)

1 NEPHI 12:19—
THE ANGEL SPEAKS TO NEPHI

A And while the **angel** spake these words,

B I beheld and saw that the **seed** of my brethren

B did contend against my **seed**,

A according to the word of the **angel**; (12:19)

1 NEPHI 13:26—
PLAIN AND PRECIOUS PARTS
OF THE GOSPEL ARE REMOVED

A **they have taken away** from the gospel of the Lamb
  B **many parts** which are plain and most precious;
  B and also **many covenants** of the Lord
A **have they taken away.** (13:26)

1 NEPHI 13:29–30—
PLAIN THINGS ARE REMOVED FROM THE BOOK

A the **Gentiles which have gone forth out of captivity**, thou seest—
  B because of the many plain and precious **things which have been taken out** of the book,
    C which were **plain** unto the understanding of the children of men,
    C according to the **plainness** which is in the Lamb of God—
  B because of these **things which are taken away out** of the gospel of the Lamb, an exceedingly great many do stumble, yea, insomuch that Satan hath great power over them. (13:29)
A Nevertheless, thou beholdest that the **Gentiles who have gone forth out of captivity**, (13:30)

1 NEPHI 13:39–42—
ALL MUST COME TO THE LAMB OF GOD

A unto the convincing of **the Gentiles** and the remnant of the seed of my brethren,
  B and also **the Jews**
    C who were scattered upon **all the face of the earth**, that the records of the prophets and of the twelve apostles of the Lamb are true. (13:39) And the angel spake unto me, saying: These last records, which thou hast seen among the Gentiles,
      D shall **establish** the truth of the first,
        E which are of the **twelve apostles of the Lamb**,

F and shall **make known** the plain and precious things which have been taken away from them; and shall make known to all kindreds, tongues, and people,

    G that **the Lamb** of God is the Son of the Eternal Father, and the Savior of the world;

        H and that all men **must come** unto him, or they cannot be saved. (13:40)

        H And they **must come** according to the words which shall be established

    G by the mouth of **the Lamb**;

F and the words of the Lamb shall be **made known** in the records of thy seed,

    E as well as in the records of the **twelve apostles of the Lamb**;

  D wherefore they both shall be **established** in one; for there is one God and one Shepherd over all the earth. (13:41)

C And the time cometh that he shall manifest himself unto **all nations**,

B both unto **the Jews**

A and also unto **the Gentiles**; (13:42)

1 NEPHI 13:42 —
THE LAMB OF GOD WILL MANIFEST
HIMSELF TO THE JEWS AND THE GENTILES

A and after he has manifested himself unto the **Jews**

  B and also unto the **Gentiles**,

  B then he shall manifest himself unto the **Gentiles**

A and also unto the **Jews**, (13:42)

1 NEPHI 13:42 —
"THE FIRST SHALL BE LAST"

A and the **last**

  B shall be **first**,

  B and the **first**

A shall be **last**. (13:42)

1 Nephi 14:15–16—
God's Wrath upon the Abominable Church

A And it came to pass that **I beheld**

  B that the **wrath of God** was poured out

    C upon that **great and abominable church,**

      D insomuch that there were **wars and rumors of wars among all the nations** and kindreds of the earth. (14:15)

      D And as there began to be **wars and rumors of wars among all the nations**

    C which belonged to the **mother of abominations,** the angel spake unto me, saying:

  B Behold, the **wrath of God** is upon the mother of harlots;

A and behold, **thou seest** all these things— (14:16)

1 Nephi 15:7–12—
How to Understand the Scriptures

A Behold, we cannot understand the words which **our father** hath spoken

  B concerning the natural branches of the **olive-tree,** and also concerning the Gentiles. (15:7) And I said unto them: Have ye inquired of the Lord? (15:8)

    C And they said unto me: We have not; for the Lord maketh no such thing **known unto us.** (15:9)

      D Behold, I said unto them: How is it that ye do not **keep the commandments of the Lord?**

        E How is it that ye will perish, because of the **hardness of your hearts?** (15:10)

          F Do ye not remember the things which the Lord hath said?—

        E If ye will not **harden your hearts,** and ask me in faith, believing that ye shall receive,

      D with diligence in **keeping my commandments,**

    C surely these things shall be made **known unto you.** (15:11)

  B Behold, I say unto you, that the house of Israel was compared unto an **olive-tree,**

A by the Spirit of the Lord which was in **our father;** (15:12)

1 NEPHI 15:25—
NEPHI EXHORTS HIS BROTHERS
TO KEEP GOD'S COMMANDMENTS

A Wherefore, I, Nephi, did exhort them to **give heed unto the word of the Lord**;

    B yea, I did exhort them with **all the energies of my soul**,

    B and with **all the faculty which I possessed**,

A that they would **give heed to the word of God** (15:25)

1 NEPHI 16:1–3—
"THE GUILTY TAKETH THE TRUTH TO BE HARD"

A **Thou hast declared unto us hard things**, more than we are able to bear. (16:1)

    B And it came to pass that I said unto them that I knew that I had spoken hard things against the wicked, according to **the truth**;

        C and the **righteous** have I justified,

            D and testified that **they should be lifted up** at the last day;

                E wherefore, the guilty taketh the **truth to be hard**,

                E for **it cutteth them** to the very center. (16:2)

            D And now my brethren, if **ye were righteous** and were willing to hearken to the truth, and give heed unto it,

        C that ye might **walk uprightly** before God,

    B then ye would not murmur because of **the truth**, and say:

A **Thou speakest hard things against us**. (16:3)

1 NEPHI 16:28–29—
THE LIAHONA WORKS ACCORDING
TO ONE'S "FAITH AND DILIGENCE"

A I, Nephi, beheld the **pointers** which were in the ball,

    B that they did work **according to the faith and diligence** and heed which we did give unto them. (16:28)

        C And there was also **written** upon them a new writing,

            D **which was plain to be read**,

            D **which did give us understanding** concerning the ways of the Lord;

C and it was **written** and changed from time to time,

   B **according to the faith and diligence** which we gave unto it.

A And thus we see that by **small means** the Lord can bring about great things. (16:29)

1 NEPHI 17:13—
WHEN WE KEEP GOD'S COMMANDMENTS, HE IS OUR LIGHT

A And **I will also be your light** in the wilderness;

   B and I will **prepare the way** before you,

      C if it so be that ye shall **keep my commandments**;

      C wherefore, inasmuch as ye shall **keep my commandments**

   B ye shall **be led** towards the promised land;

A and ye shall know that **it is by me that ye are led**. (17:13)

1 NEPHI 17:17–19—
NEPHI'S BROTHERS CONDEMN HIM

A Our brother is a **fool**,

   B for he thinketh that he can **build a ship**; yea, and he also thinketh that he can cross these great waters. (17:17)

      C And thus my **brethren did complain against me**, and were desirous that they might not labor, for they did not believe that I could build a ship; neither would they believe that I was instructed of the Lord. (17:18) And now it came to pass that

         D I, Nephi, was exceedingly **sorrowful** because of the **hardness of their hearts**;

         D and now when they saw that I began to be **sorrowful** they were **glad in their hearts**,

      C insomuch that **they did rejoice over me**, saying:

   B We knew that ye could not **construct a ship**,

A for we knew that ye were **lacking in judgment**; wherefore, thou canst not accomplish so great a work. (17:19)

1 Nephi 17:31—
The Lord Did All Things for Moses and Israel

A and according to **his word**
  B he did **do all things** for them;
  B and there was **not any thing done**
A save it were by **his word**. (17:31)

1 Nephi 17:38—
The Lord Leads the Righteous
and Destroys the Wicked

A And **he leadeth** away
  B the **righteous** into precious lands,
  B and the **wicked**
A **he destroyeth**, (17:38)

1 Nephi 17:46—
The Awesome Power of God's Word

A yea, and ye know that by his word he can cause the **rough** places
  B to be made **smooth**,
  B and **smooth** places
A shall be **broken up**.

1 Nephi 17:48-52—
Nephi Commands His Brothers Not to Touch Him

A and as they came forth to **lay their hands upon me**
  B **I spake unto them, saying**:
    C In the name of the Almighty God, I command you that ye touch me not, for I am filled with the **power of God**, even unto the consuming of my flesh; and whoso shall lay his hands upon me shall wither even as a dried reed; and he shall be as naught before the **power of God**, for God shall smite him. (17:48)
      D And it came to pass that I, Nephi, said unto them that they should murmur no more against their father; neither should

they withhold their labor from me, for **God had commanded me** that I should build a ship. (17:49)

    E And I said unto them: If **God had commanded me** to do all things I could do them.

    D If **he should command me** that I should say unto this water, be thou earth, it should be earth; and if I should say it, it would be done. (17:50)

  C And now, if the **Lord has such great power**, and has wrought so many miracles among the children of men, how is it that he cannot instruct me, that I should build a ship? (17:51)

 B And it came to pass that **I, Nephi, said many things unto my brethren**,

A insomuch that they were confounded and could not contend against me; neither durst they **lay their hands upon me** nor touch me with their fingers, (17:52)

1 NEPHI 18:24—
NEPHI AND HIS FAMILY PLANT
SEEDS IN THE PROMISED LAND

A And it came to pass that we did begin to till the **earth**,

 B and we began to plant **seeds**;

 B yea, we did put all our **seeds**

A into the **earth**,

1 NEPHI 19:13–14—
THE PROPHET ZENOS PROPHESIES
REGARDING JESUS' CRUCIFIXION

And as for those who are at Jerusalem, saith the prophet,

 A **they shall be scourged by all people**,

  B because **they crucify the God of Israel**,

   C and **turn their hearts aside**,

    D rejecting **signs** and **wonders**,

    D and the **power** and **glory** of the God of Israel. (19:13)

   C And because they **turn their hearts aside**, saith the prophet,

  B and have **despised the Holy One of Israel**,

A **they shall** wander in the flesh, and **perish**, and become a hiss and a byword, and be hated **among all nations**. (19:14)

1 Nephi 20:21—
The Lord Caused the Rock
to Provide Water for Israel

A he caused the **waters to flow out**
  B of the **rock** for them;
  B he clave the **rock** also
A and the **waters gushed out**. (20:21)

1 Nephi 22:1–3—
Nephi Reads Things that Pertain
to the Spiritual and the Temporal

A What meaneth these things which ye **have read**? Behold, are they to be understood **according to things** which are **spiritual**,
  B **which shall come** to pass according to the spirit and not **the flesh**? (22:1)
    C And I, Nephi, said unto them: Behold they were **manifest unto the prophet**
      D by the voice of **the Spirit**;
      D for by **the Spirit**
    C are all things made **known unto the prophets**,
  B **which shall come** upon the children of men according to **the flesh**. (22:2)
A Wherefore, the things of which I **have read** are things **pertaining to things** both temporal and **spiritual**; (22:3)

1 Nephi 22:25—
The Lord Numbers His Sheep

A and he numbereth **his sheep**, and they know him;
  B and there shall be **one** fold
  B and **one** shepherd;
A and he shall feed **his sheep**, and in him they shall find pasture. (22:5)

1 Nephi 22:26—
The Power of Righteousness

A And because of the **righteousness** of his people,

    B Satan has **no power**;

        C wherefore, **he cannot be loosed** for the space of many years;

    B for he hath **no power** over the hearts of the people,

A for they dwell in **righteousness**, (22:26)

2 Nephi

A O that ye would **awake**; awake from a deep sleep, yea, even from the sleep of hell , and shake off the awful **chains by which ye are bound**, which are the chains which bind the children of men,

> **B** that they are carried away captive down to the **eternal gulf of misery and woe**. (1:13)

>> **C** Awake! and **arise from the dust**, and hear the words of a trembling parent,

>>> **D** whose limbs ye must soon lay down in the cold and silent **grave**, from whence no traveler can return; a few more days and I go the way of all the earth. (1:14)

>>>> **E** But behold, the Lord hath redeemed **my soul** from hell; I have beheld his glory, and I am encircled about eternally in the arms of his love. (1:15)

>>>>> **F** And I desire that ye should remember to **observe the statutes and the judgments** of the Lord; behold, this hath been the anxiety of my soul from the beginning. (1:16) My heart hath been weighed down with sorrow from time to time, for I have feared, lest for the hardness of your hearts the Lord your God should come out in the fulness of his wrath upon you, that ye be **cut off** and destroyed forever; (1:17)

>>>>>> **G** Or, that a cursing should come upon you for the space of many generations; and ye are **visited by sword, and by famine, and are hated, and are led**

according to the will and captivity of the devil. (1:18)

    G O my sons, that **these things** might not come upon you, but that ye might be a choice and a favored people of the Lord. But behold, his will be done; for his ways are righteousness forever. (1:19)

  F And he hath said that: Inasmuch as ye shall **keep my commandments** ye shall prosper in the land; but inasmuch as ye will not keep my commandments ye shall be **cut off** from my presence. (1:20)

  E And now that **my soul** might have joy in you, and that my heart might leave this world with gladness because of you,

  D that I might not be brought down with grief and sorrow to the **grave**,

 C **arise from the dust**, my sons, and be men, and be determined in one mind and in one heart, united in all things, that ye may not come down into captivity; (1:21)

B That ye may not be cursed with a sore cursing; and also, that ye may not incur the displeasure of a just God upon you, unto the destruction, yea, **the eternal destruction of both soul and body.** (1:22)

A **Awake**, my sons; put on the armor of righteousness. Shake off the **chains with which ye are bound**, and come forth out of obscurity, and arise from the dust. (1:23)

2 Nephi 1:28–29—
Lehi Leaves a Blessing upon His Sons Who Hearken unto Nephi

A I leave unto you a **blessing**,

 B yea, even my **first blessing**. (1:28)

  C But if ye will not hearken unto him

 B I take away my **first blessing**,

A yea, even my **blessing**, (1:29)

2 NEPHI 2:7—
THE IMPORTANCE OF A "BROKEN HEART" AND "CONTRITE SPIRIT"

A Behold, he offereth himself a sacrifice for sin, to **answer**
  B the **ends of the law**,
    C unto **all those**
      D who have a **broken heart**
      D and a **contrite spirit**;
    C and unto **none else**
  B can the **ends of the law**
A be **answered**.

2 NEPHI 3:1—
LEHI SPEAKS TO HIS LAST-BORN SON, JOSEPH

A Thou wast **born**
  B in the wilderness of mine **afflictions**;
  B yea, in the days of my greatest **sorrow**
A did thy **mother bear thee**. (3:1)

2 NEPHI 5:16—
NEPHI BUILDS A TEMPLE THAT IS SIMILAR TO SOLOMON'S

A And I, Nephi, did **build a temple**;
  B and I did construct it after the **manner of the temple of Solomon**
    C save it were not built of so many **precious things**;
    C for **they** were not to be found upon the land,
  B wherefore, it could not be built **like unto Solomon's temple**.
A But the manner of the **construction** was like unto the **temple** of Solomon; and the workmanship thereof was exceedingly fine. (5:16)

2 NEPHI 5:25—
A SCOURGE MOVES US TO REMEMBER GOD

And the Lord God said unto me:
  A They shall be a **scourge** unto thy seed,
    B to **stir them up**
      C in **remembrance** of me;
      C and inasmuch as they will not **remember** me,
    B and **hearken** unto my words,
  A they shall **scourge** them even unto destruction. (5:25)

2 NEPHI 6:13—
THE LORD'S PEOPLE "WAIT FOR HIM"

  A For the people of **the Lord**
    B are they who **wait** for him;
    B for they still **wait**
  A for the coming of **the Messiah**. (6:13)

2 NEPHI 6:14–15—
THOSE WHO BELIEVE IN THE MESSIAH
WILL NOT BE DESTROYED

[The Messiah] will manifest himself unto them in power and great glory, unto the destruction of their enemies, when that day cometh when they shall believe in him;
  A and none will he **destroy**
    B that **believe** in him. (6:14)
    B And they that **believe** not in him
  A shall be **destroyed**, (6:15)

2 NEPHI 9:20—
GOD KNOWS ALL THINGS

O how great the holiness of our God!
  A For **he knoweth**
    B **all things**,

B and there is **not anything**
A save **he knows** it. (9:20)

2 NEPHI 9:28—
"THE FOOLISHNESS OF MEN"

A O the vainness, and the frailties, and the **foolishness** of men!
  B When they are learned **they think they are wise,**
    C and **they hearken not** unto the counsel of God,
    C for **they set it aside,**
  B **supposing they know** of themselves,
A wherefore, their wisdom is **foolishness** and it profiteth them not.
(9:28)

2 NEPHI 9:38—
WO, IF YOU DIE IN YOUR SINS

A And, in fine, wo unto all those who die in **their sins;**
  B for they shall **return to God,**
  B and **behold his face,**
A and remain in **their sins,** (9:38)

2 NEPHI 9:42–43—
"PUFFED UP" VERSUS "DEPTHS OF HUMILITY"

A And whoso knocketh, to him **will he open;** and the **wise,** and the
learned, and they that are rich,
  B who are **puffed up**
    C because of **their learning,** and **their wisdom,**
      D and their **riches**—
        E yea, they are they whom **he despiseth;**
      D and save they shall cast **these things** away,
    C and consider **themselves fools** before God,
  B and come down in the **depths of humility,**
A **he will not open** unto them. (9:42) But the things of the **wise** and
the prudent shall be hid from them forever—(9:43)

2 Nephi 9:44–46—
The Last Day Is a Day of Judgment

A wherefore, ye shall know at **the last day**,
  B when all men shall be **judged of their works**,
    C that the **God** of Israel
      D did witness that I **shook your iniquities** from my soul,
        E and that I stand **with brightness** before him,
        E and am **rid of your blood** (9:44)
      D O, my beloved brethren, turn away from your sins; **shake off the chains** of him that would bind you fast;
    C come unto that **God** who is the rock of your salvation. (9:45)
  B Prepare your souls for that glorious day when **justice shall be administered** unto the righteous,
A even the **day of judgment**, (9:46)

2 Nephi 11:2–8—
All Things Typify Jesus Christ

And now I, Nephi, write more of the words of Isaiah, for my soul delighteth in his words.
  A For I will liken his words unto **my people**,
    B and I will send them forth unto all **my children**,
      C for he verily **saw my Redeemer**, even as I have seen him. (11:2) And my brother, Jacob, also has seen him as I have seen him; wherefore, I will send their words forth unto my children to prove unto them that my words are true.
        D Wherefore, **by the words of three**, God hath said, I will establish my word. Nevertheless, God sendeth **more witnesses**, and he proveth all his words. (11:3)
          E Behold, my soul delighteth in proving unto my people the truth of **the coming of Christ**;
            F for, for this end hath the **law of Moses been given**;
              G and **all things** which have been given of God from the beginning of the world, unto man, **are the typifying of him**, (11:4)
            F And also my soul delighteth in the **covenants of the Lord which he hath made** to our fathers; yea, my soul delighteth in his grace, and in his justice, and power, and

mercy in the great and eternal plan of deliverance from death. (11:5)

 E And my soul delighteth in proving unto my people that save **Christ should come** all men must perish. (11:6)

 D **For if there be no Christ there be no God; and if there be no God we are not, for there could have been no creation, But there is a God,**

 C and **he is Christ**, and he cometh in the fulness of his own time. (11:7)

B And now I write some of the words of Isaiah, that whoso of **my people** shall see these words may lift up their hearts and rejoice for all men.

A Now these are the words, and **ye may liken them unto you** and unto all men. (11:8)

2 Nephi 25:4—
Hearken to Nephi's Words

A Wherefore, **hearken**,

 B O my **people**,

 B which are of the **house of Israel**,

A and **give ear** unto my words; (25:4)

2 Nephi 25:15—
Jews Will Be Scattered, Babylon Destroyed

A Wherefore, the **Jews shall be scattered** among all nations;

 B yea, and also **Babylon shall be destroyed**;

A wherefore, the **Jews shall be scattered** by other nations. (25:15)

2 Nephi 25:24–27—
The Deadness of the Law versus Life in Christ

A And, notwithstanding we believe in Christ, **we keep the law of Moses,**

 B and look forward with steadfastness unto Christ, until the **law shall be fulfilled.** (25:24)

C For, for **this end was the law given**;

    D wherefore the **law hath become dead** unto us, and we are **made alive in Christ** because of our faith; yet we keep the law because of the commandments. (25:25)

        E And we talk of Christ, we rejoice in Christ, we preach of Christ, we **prophesy** of Christ,

        E and we write according to our **prophecies**, that our children may know to what source they may look for a remission of their sins. (25:26) Wherefore, we speak concerning the law that our children may know

    D the **deadness of the law**; and they, by knowing the **deadness of the law**, may look forward unto that **life which is in Christ**,

  C and know for **what end the law was given**.

 B And after **the law is fulfilled** in Christ,

A that they need not harden their hearts against him when **the law ought to be done away**. (25:27)

2 NEPHI 26:1–9— THE RESURRECTED JESUS CHRIST WILL APPEAR TO THE RIGHTEOUS

A And after Christ shall have risen from the dead **he shall show himself unto you**, my children, and my beloved brethren;

 B and the **words which he shall speak unto you shall be the law which ye shall do**, (26:1)

  C For behold, I say unto you that **I have beheld** that many generations shall pass away,

    D and there shall be great **wars and contentions among my people**. (26:2)

        E And after the Messiah shall come there shall be **signs given unto my people** of his birth, and also of his death and resurrection; and **great and terrible shall that day be** unto the wicked,

           F for **they shall perish; and they perish**

                G because **they cast out the prophets, and the saints**, and stone them, and slay them; wherefore the cry of the blood of the saints shall ascend up to God from the ground against them. (26:3)

H Wherefore, all those who are proud, and that do wickedly, the day that cometh shall **burn them up**,

H saith the Lord of Hosts, for they shall **be as stubble**, (26:4)

G And **they that kill the prophets, and the saints,**

F the depths of the earth shall **swallow them up**, saith the Lord of Hosts; and mountains shall **cover them**, and whirlwinds shall **carry them away**, and buildings shall **fall upon them** and **crush them to pieces** and **grind them to powder**. (26:5)

E And they shall be **visited with thunderings**, and **lightnings**, and **earthquakes**, and **all manner of destructions**, for the fire of the anger of the Lord shall be kindled against them, and they shall be as stubble, and the day that cometh shall consume them, saith the Lord of Hosts. (26:6)

D O the pain, and the anguish of my soul for the loss of the **slain of my people!**

C For **I, Nephi, have seen it**, and it well nigh consumeth me before the presence of the Lord; but I must cry unto my God: Thy ways are just. (26:7)

B But behold, the **righteous that hearken unto the words of the prophets**, and destroy them not, but look forward unto Christ with steadfastness for the signs which are given, notwithstanding all persecution—behold, they are they which shall not perish. (26:8)

A But the **Son of righteousness shall appear unto them**; (26:9)

2 NEPHI 27:1–4—
REGARDING NATIONS THAT FIGHT AGAINST ZION

A behold, **they will be drunken**

B **with iniquity** and all manner of abominations—(27:1) And when that day shall come they shall be visited of the Lord of Hosts, with thunder and with earthquake, and with a great noise, and with storm, and with tempest, and with the flame of devouring fire. (27:2)

C And **all the nations that fight against Zion**, and that distress her, shall be as a dream of a night vision; yea, it shall be unto them,

D even as unto a **hungry man which dreameth**, and behold he eateth but he awaketh and his soul is empty;

   D or like unto a **thirsty man which dreameth**, and behold he drinketh but he awaketh and behold he is faint, and his soul hath appetite;

  C yea, even so shall the multitude of **all the nations be that fight against Mount Zion.** (27:3)

 B For behold, **all ye that doeth iniquity**, stay yourselves and wonder, for ye shall cry out, and cry;

A yea, **ye shall be drunken** but not with wine, ye shall stagger but not with strong drink. (27:4)

2 NEPHI 28:3—
CHURCHES THAT "ARE NOT UNTO THE LORD"

For it shall come to pass in that day
  A that the **churches which are built up**, and **not unto the Lord**,
    B when the **one shall say** unto the other:
      C Behold, **I, I am the Lord's**;
      C and the others shall say: **I, I am the Lord's**;
    B and thus **shall every one say**
  A that **hath built up churches**, and **not unto the Lord.** (28:3)

2 NEPHI 28:21—
"ALL IS WELL IN ZION"

A And **others will he pacify,**
  B and **lull them away** into carnal security,
    C that they will say: **All is well**
      D in **Zion**;
      D yea, **Zion** prospereth,
    C **all is well**—
  B and thus the **devil cheateth their souls,**
A and **leadeth them away** carefully down to hell. (28:21)

2 Nephi 28:32—
God Is Merciful to the Repentant

A Wo be unto the Gentiles, **saith the Lord God of Hosts**!

  B For notwithstanding I shall **lengthen out mine arm** unto them from **day to day**

    C they will **deny me**;

      D nevertheless, I will be **merciful** unto them, saith the Lord God, if they will **repent**

    C and **come unto me**;

  B for **mine arm is lengthened** out all the **day** long,

A **saith the Lord God of Hosts**. (28:32)

2 Nephi 29:3–6—
Some Will Say, "We Need No More Bible"

A A Bible! **A Bible! We have got a Bible**, and there cannot be **any more Bible**. (29:3)

  B But thus saith the Lord God: O **fools**, they shall have a Bible;

  C and it shall proceed forth from the Jews, **mine** ancient covenant **people**.

    D And **what thank they the Jews** for the Bible which they receive from them?

      E Yea, **what do the Gentiles mean**?

        G **Do they remember** the travails, and the labors, and the pains of **the Jews**, and their diligence unto me,

          H in bringing forth salvation unto the **Gentiles**? (29:4)

          H O ye **Gentiles**,

        G **have ye remembered the Jews**, mine ancient covenant people?

      E Nay; but ye **have cursed them**, and **have hated them**, and have not sought to recover them.

    D But behold, **I will return all these things upon your own heads**;

  C for I the Lord have not forgotten **my people**. (29:5)

  B Thou **fool**, that shall say:

A A **Bible, we have got a Bible**, and we need **no more Bible**. (29:6)

2 Nephi 29:13—
Scriptures of the Jews and the Nephites

A And it shall come to pass that the **Jews**
  B shall have the **words**
    C of the **Nephites**,
    C and the **Nephites**
  B shall have the **words**
A of the **Jews**; (29:13)

2 Nephi 29:13—
Scriptures of the Lost Tribes of Israel

A and the **Nephites and the Jews**
  B shall have the **words**
    C of the **lost tribes of Israel**;
    C and the **lost tribes of Israel**
  B shall have the **words**
A of the **Nephites and the Jews**. (29:13)

2 Nephi 32:2—
Speaking with the Tongue of Angels

A that after ye had received the **Holy Ghost**
  B ye could speak with the **tongue of angels**?
  B And now, how could ye speak with the **tongue of angels**
A save it were by the **Holy Ghost**? (32:2)

Jacob

A Wherefore, the people were desirous to retain in remembrance his **name**.
   B And whoso should **reign** in his stead were **called by the people**,
      C **second Nephi**,
      C **third Nephi**, and so forth,
   B according to the **reigns** of the kings; and thus they were **called by the people**,
A let them be of whatever **name** they would. (1:11)

But I, Jacob, shall not hereafter distinguish them by these names,
   A but **I shall call** them **Lamanites**
      B that seek to **destroy the people of Nephi**,
      B and those who are **friendly to Nephi**
   A **I shall call Nephites**, (1:14)

A Yea, it grieveth my soul and **causeth me to shrink with shame**
   B **before the presence** of my Maker,

C that I must testify unto you concerning the **wickedness of your hearts**. (2:6)

    D And also it grieveth me that **I must use** so much boldness of speech concerning you,

        E before your wives and your children, many of **whose feelings are exceedingly tender and chaste and delicate** before God, which thing is pleasing unto God; (2:7)

            F And it supposeth me that they have come up hither to hear the **pleasing word of God**,

                G yea, the word which **healeth the wounded soul**. (2:8)

                    H Wherefore, it burdeneth my soul that I should be constrained, because of the strict commandment which I have received from God, **to admonish you** according to your crimes,

                        I to enlarge the **wounds**

                        I of those who are already **wounded**,

                    H **instead of consoling**

                G and **healing their wounds**;

            F and those who have not been wounded, instead of feasting upon the **pleasing word of God**

        E have daggers placed to pierce their souls and wound their **delicate minds**. (2:9)

    D But, notwithstanding the greatness of the task, **I must do** according to the strict commands of God,

  C and tell you concerning **your wickedness** and abominations,

 B **in the presence** of the pure in heart, and the broken heart,

A and **under the glance of the piercing eye** of the Almighty God. (2:10)

JACOB 3:6—
KEEPING THE LORD'S COMMANDMENT

A And now, this **commandment**

 B they **observe** to keep;

 B wherefore, because of this **observance**,

A in keeping this **commandment**, (3:6)

JACOB 4:9—
GOD CREATED THE EARTH BY HIS POWER

A For behold, by the **power of his word**

    B man came upon the face of the **earth**,

    B which **earth**

A was created by the **power of his word**. (4:9)

JACOB 5:61–64—
PREPARING THE VINEYARD FOR THE LAST TIME

A Wherefore, go to, and call servants, that we may labor diligently with our might in the vineyard, that **we may prepare the way**,

    B that **I may bring forth again the natural fruit**, which natural fruit is good and the most precious above all other fruit. (5:61)

        C Wherefore, let us go to and labor with our might this **last time**, for behold the **end draweth nigh**, and this is for the **last time** that I shall **prune my vineyard**. (5:62)

            D Graft in the branches; begin at the **last** that they may be **first**, and that the **first** may be **last**,

            D and dig about the trees, both old and young, the **first** and the **last**; and the **last** and the **first**,

        C that all may be nourished once again for the **last time**. (5:63) Wherefore, dig about them, and **prune them**, and dung them once more, for the **last time**, for the **end draweth nigh**.

    B And if it be so that these last grafts shall grow, and **bring forth the natural fruit**,

A then **shall ye prepare the way** for them, that they may grow. (5:64)

Enos, Omni, and Words of Mormon

ENOS 1:8–12 —
ENOS'S GREAT FAITH IN JESUS CHRIST

A And he said unto me: **Because of thy faith** in Christ, whom thou hast never before heard nor seen. And many years pass away before he shall manifest himself in the flesh; wherefore, go to, thy faith hath made thee whole. (1:8)

> **B** Now, it came to pass that **when I had heard these words** I began to feel a desire for the welfare of **my brethren, the Nephites**; wherefore, **I did pour out my whole soul unto God for them**. (1:9)

> > **C** And while I was thus struggling in the spirit, behold, the voice of the Lord came into my mind again, saying: **I will visit thy brethren according to their diligence** in keeping my commandments.

> > > **D** I have given unto them this **land**,

> > > **D** and it is a holy **land**; and I curse it not save it be for the cause of iniquity;

> > **C** wherefore, **I will visit thy brethren according as I have said**; and their transgressions will I bring down with sorrow upon their own heads. (1:10)

> **B** And **after I, Enos, had heard these words**, my faith began to be unshaken in the Lord; and **I prayed unto him with many long strugglings** for **my brethren, the Lamanites**. (1:11)

A And it came to pass that after I had prayed and labored with all diligence, the Lord said unto me: I will grant unto thee according to thy desires, **because of thy faith**. (1:12)

Enos 1:13–16—
Enos Prays that God Would Preserve the Records

And now behold, this was the desire which I desired of him . . .
A that the **Lord God would preserve a record** of my people, the Nephites; even if it so be by the power of his holy arm, that it might be **brought forth at some future day unto the Lamanites**, that, perhaps, they might be brought unto salvation— (1:13)

    B For at the present our strugglings were vain in restoring them to the **true faith**.

        C And they swore in their wrath that, if it were possible, they would **destroy our records** and us, and also all the traditions of our fathers. (1:14)

        C Wherefore, I knowing that the Lord God was able to **preserve our records**, I cried unto him continually, for he had said unto me: Whatsoever thing ye shall ask in faith, believing that ye shall receive in the name of Christ, ye shall receive it. (1:15)

    B And I had **faith**,

A and I did cry unto God that **he would preserve the records**; and he covenanted with me that he would **bring them forth unto the Lamanites** in his own due time. (1:16)

Omni 1:12–13—
The Lord Warns Mosiah

A Behold, I will speak unto you somewhat concerning Mosiah, who was made king over the **land of Zarahemla**;

    B for behold, he being **warned of the Lord**

        C that he should **flee** out of the land of Nephi,

            D and as many as would **hearken unto the voice of the Lord**

                E should also **depart** out of the land with him, into the **wilderness**— (1:12)

                    F And it came to pass that **he did**

                    F according **as the Lord had commanded him.**

                E And they **departed** out of the land into the **wilderness**,

            D as many as would **hearken unto the voice of the Lord**;

        C and they were **led** by many preachings and prophesyings.

B And they were **admonished** continually **by the word of God**; and they were led by the power of his arm, through the wilderness,

A until they came down into the land which is called the **land of Zarahemla**. (1:13)

OMNI 1:14—
GREAT REJOICING IN ZARAHEMLA

A Now, there was **great rejoicing**
  B among the people of **Zarahemla**;
  B and also **Zarahemla**
A did **rejoice exceedingly**,

WORDS OF MORMON 1:5–9—
MORMON FINISHES HIS RECORD

A Wherefore, **I** chose these things, **to finish my record** upon them, which remainder of my record **I shall take from the plates of Nephi**; and I cannot write the hundredth part of the things of my people. (1:5)
  B But behold, I shall take these plates, which contain these prophesyings and revelations, and put them with the remainder of my record, for they are choice unto me; and I know they will be choice unto **my brethren**. (1:6)
    C And I do this for a wise purpose; for thus it whispereth me, according to the **workings of the Spirit** of the Lord which is **in me**.
      D And now, **I do not know all things**;
      D but the **Lord knoweth all things** which are to come;
    C wherefore, he **worketh in me** to do according to his will. (1:7)
  B And my prayer to God is concerning **my brethren**, that they may once again come to the knowledge of God, yea, the redemption of Christ; that they may once again be a delightsome people. (1:8)
A And now I, **Mormon**, proceed **to finish out my record**, which **I take from the plates of Nephi**; and I make it according to the knowledge and the understanding which God has given me. (1:9)

Mosiah

MOSIAH 2:5–6—
FAMILIES PITCH THEIR TENTS AROUND THE TEMPLE

A And it came to pass that when they came up to the **temple**,
  B **they pitched their tents round about**,
    C every man according to his **family**,
      D consisting of his wife, and his **sons**, and his **daughters**,
      D and their **sons**, and their **daughters**, from the eldest down
      to the youngest,
    C every **family** being separate one from another. (2:5)
  B And **they pitched their tents round about**
A the **temple**, (2:6)

MOSIAH 2:7–8—
BENJAMIN CAUSES A TOWER TO BE ERECTED

A For the **multitude** being so **great**
  B that king Benjamin **could not teach them all** within the walls of
  the temple,
    C therefore he caused a **tower** to be erected,
      D that thereby his **people** might hear the words
        E which he should **speak** unto them. (2:7)
        E And it came to pass that he began to **speak**
      D to his **people**
    C from the **tower**;
  B and they **could not all hear** his words
A because of the **greatness** of the **multitude**; (2:8)

MOSIAH 2:15–16—
BENJAMIN DOES NOT DESIRE TO BOAST

A Yet, my brethren, I have not done these things that I might **boast**,

    B neither do **I tell these things** that thereby I might accuse you;

    B but **I tell you these things** that ye may know that I can answer a clear conscience before God this day. (2:15)

A Behold, I say unto you that because I said unto you that I had spent my days in your service, **I do not desire to boast**, for I have only been in the service of God (2:16)

MOSIAH 2:25—
WE ARE CREATED FROM THE DUST

A yet ye were **created**

    B of the **dust** of the earth;

    B but behold, **it** belongeth to him

A who **created** you.

MOSIAH 2:26—
BENJAMIN IS FROM THE DUST

A for I am also of the **dust**.

    B And ye behold that **I am old**,

    B and **am about to yield up this mortal frame**

A to its **mother earth**.

MOSIAH 3:1–3—
AN ANGEL REVEALS GLAD TIDINGS TO BENJAMIN

A for behold, I have things **to tell you** concerning

    B that which is to **come**. (3:1)

        C And the things which **I shall tell you**

            D are **made known unto me** by an angel from God.

                E And he said unto me: **Awake**;

                    F **and I awoke**, and behold he stood before me. (3:2)

                E And he said unto me: **Awake**,

      D and **hear the words**
    C which **I shall tell thee;**
  B for behold, I am **come**
A **to declare unto you** the glad tidings of great joy. (3:3)

MOSIAH 3:11–16—
JESUS CHRIST'S BLOOD ATONES FOR OUR SINS

A For behold, and also **his blood atoneth** for the sins
  B of those who have **fallen** by the transgression of **Adam,**
    C who have died not knowing the will of God concerning them,
    or who have **ignorantly sinned.** (3:11)
      D But wo, wo unto him who knoweth that he **rebelleth against God**! For salvation cometh to none such except it be through repentance and faith on the Lord Jesus Christ. (3:12)
        E And the Lord God hath sent his **holy prophets** among all the children of men, to declare these things to every kindred, nation, and tongue, that thereby whosoever should believe **that Christ should come**, the same might receive remission of their sins, and rejoice with exceedingly great joy, even as though he had already come among them. (3:13) Yet the Lord God saw that his people were a stiffnecked people,
          F and **he appointed unto them** a law,
          F even the **law of Moses.** (3:14) And many signs, and wonders, and types, and shadows
        E showed he unto them, concerning his **coming**; and also **holy prophets** spake unto them **concerning his coming;**
      D and yet they **hardened their hearts,** and understood not that the law of Moses availeth nothing except it were through the atonement of his blood. (3:15)
    C And even **if it were possible that little children could sin** they could not be saved; but I say unto you they are blessed;
  B for behold, as in **Adam**, or by nature, they **fall,**
A even so the **blood of Christ atoneth** for their sins. (3:16)

Mosiah 3:18–19—
The Natural Man Can Become a Saint
through Christ's Atonement

A but men drink damnation to their own souls except they **humble** themselves

  B and become as little **children**,

    C and believe that salvation was, and is, and is to come, in and through the **atoning blood of Christ**, the Lord Omnipotent. (3:18)

      D For the **natural man**

        E is an enemy to **God**,

          F and **has been** from the fall of Adam,

          F and **will be**, forever and ever,

        E unless he yields to the enticings of the **Holy Spirit**,

      D and putteth off the **natural man**

    C and becometh a saint through the **atonement of Christ** the Lord,

  B and becometh as a **child**,

A submissive, meek, **humble**, patient, full of love, willing to submit to all things which the Lord seeth fit to inflict upon him, even as a child doth submit to his father. (3:19)

Mosiah 4:6–7—
The Atonement Was Prepared
from the World's Foundation

A and also, the **atonement** which has been **prepared from the foundation of the world**,

  B that thereby **salvation might come to him**

    C that should put his **trust** in the Lord,

      D and should **be diligent**

      D in **keeping** his **commandments**,

    C and continue in the **faith** even unto the end of his life, I mean the life of the mortal body— (4:6)

  B I say, that this is the **man who receiveth salvation**,

A through the **atonement** which was **prepared from the foundation of the world**. (4:7)

MOSIAH 4:11–12—
TASTING OF GOD'S LOVE

A and have tasted of **his love**, and have received a **remission of your sins**,

    B which causeth such exceedingly great **joy in your souls**, even so I would that ye should remember, and always retain in remembrance, the greatness of God,

        C and **your own nothingness**, and his goodness and long-suffering towards you, **unworthy creatures**,

        C and **humble yourselves** even in the **depths of humility**, calling on the name of the Lord daily, and standing steadfastly in the faith of that which is to come, which was spoken by the mouth of the angel. (4:11)

    B And behold, I say unto you that if ye do this **ye shall always rejoice**,

A and be filled with the **love of God**, and always retain a **remission of your sins**; (4:12)

MOSIAH 4:14–15—
TEACH CHILDREN TO WALK IN THE WAYS OF TRUTH

A And **ye will not suffer your children** that they go hungry, or naked;

    B neither will ye **suffer that they transgress the laws of God**,

        C and **fight** and quarrel one with another,

            D and serve the **devil**,

                E who is the **master of sin**,

                E or who is the **evil spirit**

            D **which hath been spoken of** by our fathers,

        C he being an **enemy** to all righteousness. (4:14)

    B But **ye will teach them to walk in the ways of truth** and soberness;

A **ye will teach them** to love one another, and to serve one another. (4:15)

MOSIAH 4:20—
THE SPIRIT GIVES US JOY

[H]e has poured out his Spirit upon you,

  A and has caused that **your hearts should be filled with joy,**

    B and has caused that **your mouths should be stopped**

    B that **ye could not find utterance,**

  A so **exceedingly great was your joy.** (4:20)

MOSIAH 5:8–9—
THE NAME OF CHRIST

A There is no other **name** given whereby salvation cometh;

  B therefore, I would that ye should take upon you the **name of Christ,**

    C all you that have entered into the **covenant with God**

      D that ye should be **obedient** unto the end of your lives. (5:8)

      D And it shall come to pass that whosoever **doeth this**

    C shall be found at the **right hand of God,**

  B for he shall know the **name by which he is called;**

A for he shall be called by the **name** of Christ. (5:9)

MOSIAH 5:10–12—
TAKE ON THE NAME OF CHRIST

And now it shall come to pass,

  A that whosoever shall not take upon him the **name of Christ**

    B must be **called** by some other name;

      C therefore, he findeth himself on the **left hand of God.** (5:10)

      D And I would that ye should **remember** also, that this is the name

        E that I said I should give unto you that never should be **blotted out,**

          F except it be through **transgression**; therefore,

          F take heed that ye do not **transgress,**

        E that the name be not **blotted out** of your hearts. (5:11)

      D I say unto you, I would that ye should **remember** to retain the name

    C written always in your hearts, that ye are not found on the **left hand of God**,

    B but that ye hear and know the voice by which ye shall be **called**,

A and also, the **name** by which he shall call you. (5:12)

MOSIAH 7:4—
SIXTEEN STRONG MEN WANDER IN THE WILDERNESS

A therefore **they wandered**

    B **many days** in the wilderness,

    B even **forty days**

A did **they wander**. (7:4)

MOSIAH 7:7–8—
STANDING BEFORE THE KING

And behold, they met the king of the people who were in the land of Nephi, and in the land of Shilom;

    A and they were **surrounded by the king's guard**,

        B and were **taken**, and **were bound**,

            C and were committed to **prison**. (7:7)

            C And it came to pass when they had been in **prison** two days

        B they were again **brought** before the king, and their **bands were loosed**;

A and they **stood before the king**, (7:8)

MOSIAH 10:17—
CONCERNING TEACHING CHILDREN HATRED

A And thus they have taught their **children**

    B that they should **hate** them,

        C and that they should **murder** them,

            D and that they should **rob**

            D and **plunder** them

        C and do all they could to **destroy** them;

    B therefore they have an eternal **hatred**

A towards the **children** of Nephi. (10:17)

MOSIAH 11:20-25—
REPENT OR BE SMITTEN

A Behold, thus saith the Lord, and **thus hath he commanded me**, saying, Go forth, and say unto this people,

    B thus saith the Lord—

        C Wo be unto this people, for **I have seen their abominations**, and their wickedness, and their whoredoms;

            D and except they repent I will visit them in mine anger. (11:20)

                E And except they repent and turn to the Lord their God, behold, I will deliver them **into the hands of their enemies**; yea, and they shall be brought into bondage; and they shall be afflicted by the hand of their enemies. (11:21)

                    F And it shall come to pass that **they shall know that I am the Lord their God**

                        G and am a jealous God, **visiting the iniquities** of my people. (11:22)

                            H And it shall come to pass that except this people **repent**

                            H and **turn unto the Lord** their God

                        G they shall be **brought into bondage**;

                    F and **none shall deliver them, except it be the Lord the Almighty God** (11:23)

                E Yea, and it shall come to pass that when they shall cry unto me I will be slow to hear their cries; yea, and I will suffer them that they be **smitten by their enemies**. (11:24)

            D And except they repent in sackcloth and ashes, and cry mightily to the Lord their God

        C I will not hear their prayers, neither will I deliver them out of their afflictions;

    B and **thus saith the Lord,**

A and **thus hath he commanded me**. (11:25)

MOSIAH 11:28—
KING NOAH DESIRES TO SLAY ABINADI

I command you to bring Abinadi hither,
  A that I may **slay him**,
    B for he has said these things that he might stir up **my people**
      C to **anger one with another**,
      C and to **raise contentions**
    B among **my people**;
  A therefore I will **slay him**. (11:28)

MOSIAH 12:1–8—
ABINADI PROPHESIES

Thus has the Lord commanded me, saying—
  A **Abinadi**, go and **prophesy** unto **this** my **people**, for they have hardened their hearts against my words;
    B **they have repented not** of their evil doings; therefore,
      a I will **visit** them
        b in my anger,
        b yea, in **my** fierce **anger**
      a will I **visit** them
    C in their **iniquities and abominations**. (12:1)
      D Yea, wo be unto this generation! And the Lord said unto me: Stretch forth thy hand and prophesy saying: Thus saith the Lord, **it shall come to pass** that this generation,
        E because of their iniquities, shall be brought into bondage, and shall be **smitten** on the cheek;
          F yea, and shall be driven by men, and shall be slain; and the vultures of the air, and the dogs, yea, and the wild beasts, shall **devour** their flesh. (12:2) And it shall come to pass that the life of king Noah shall be valued even as a garment in a hot furnace; for he shall know that I am the Lord. (12:3)
            G And it shall come to pass that I will smite this my people with sore afflictions, yea, with famine and with **pestilence**; and I will cause that they shall howl all the day long. (12:4)

H Yea, and I will cause that they shall have **burdens lashed upon their backs**;

H and they shall be driven before **like a dumb ass**. (12:5)

G And it shall come to pass that I will send forth hail among them, and it shall smite them; and they shall also be smitten with the east wind; and **insects shall pester** their land also,

F and **devour** their grain. (12:6)

E And they shall be **smitten** with a great pestilence—

D and all **this will I do**

C because of their **iniquities and abominations**. (12:7)

B And it shall come to pass that **except they repent** I will utterly destroy them from off the face of the earth; yet they shall leave a record behind them, and I will preserve them for other nations which shall possess the land; yea, even this will I do that I may discover the abominations of this people to other nations.

A And many things did **Abinadi prophesy** against **this people**. (12:8)

MOSIAH 12:19—
ABINADI ASTONISHES THE PRIESTS WITH HIS RESPONSES

And they began to question him, that they might cross him, that thereby they might have wherewith to accuse him;

A but **he answered them** boldly,

B and **withstood all their questions**,

C yea, to **their astonishment**;

B for he did **withstand** them in **all their questions**,

A and **did confound them** in all their words. (12:19)

MOSIAH 12:25-27—
ABINADI CONDEMNS THE PRIESTS

And now Abinadi said unto them:

A Are you priests, and pretend to **teach this people**,

B and to **understand** the spirit of prophesying, and yet desire to know of me what these things mean? (12:25)

C I say unto you, wo be unto you for **perverting the ways of the Lord!**

    D For if ye understand **these things**

    D ye have not taught **them**;

C therefore, ye have **perverted the ways of the Lord** (12:26)

B Ye have not applied your hearts to **understanding**;

A therefore, ye have not been wise. Therefore, what **teach** ye **this people?** (12:27)

MOSIAH 15:20–23—
ABINADI TEACHES CONCERNING
CHRIST AND THE RESURRECTION

A But behold, the **bands of death**

  B shall be **broken,**

    C and the **Son** reigneth,

      D and hath **power over the dead**;

        E therefore, he bringeth to pass the **resurrection of the dead** (15:20)

          F And there cometh a **resurrection,**

           G even a **first resurrection**;

             H yea, even a resurrection of **those that have been**, and **who are**, and **who shall be,**

               I even until the **resurrection**

                 J of **Christ**—

                 J for **so shall he be called** (15:21)

               I And now, the **resurrection**

             H of **all the prophets**, and **all those that have believed** in their words, or **all those that have kept the commandments** of God,

           G shall come forth in the **first resurrection**;

          F therefore, they are the first **resurrection.** (15:22)

        E They are **raised** to dwell with God who has redeemed them;

      D thus they have **eternal life**

    C through **Christ,**

  B who has **broken**

A the **bands of death.** (15:23)

Mosiah 15:26–27—
Wicked Priests Tremble before God

But behold, and fear, and tremble before God,
A for ye **ought to tremble**;
   B for the Lord **redeemeth none such**
      C that **rebel against him**
         D and **die in their sins**;
         D yea, even all those that have **perished in their sins** ever since the world began,
      C that have wilfully **rebelled against God**, that have known the commandments of God, and would not keep them;
   B these are they that have **no part in the first resurrection**. (15:26)
A Therefore **ought** ye not **to tremble**? (15:27)

Mosiah 16:7–8—
Death's Sting "Is Swallowed Up in Christ"

A And if **Christ** had not risen from the dead, or have broken the bands of death
   B that the **grave** should have no **victory**, and that **death** should have no **sting**,
      C there could have been no **resurrection**. (16:7)
      C But there is a **resurrection**,
   B therefore the **grave** hath no **victory**, and the **sting** of **death**
A is swallowed up in **Christ**. (16:8)

Mosiah 18:21—
Alma Teaches Unity among the Saints

A And he commanded them that there should be **no contention one with another**,
   B but that they should look forward with **one eye**,
      C having **one faith**
      C and **one baptism**,
   B having their **hearts** knit together **in unity**
A and in **love one towards another**. (18:21)

MOSIAH 23:7—
ALMA TEACHES AGAINST KINGSHIP

A Behold, it is **not expedient that we should have a king;**
  B for thus **saith the Lord:**
    C Ye shall not **esteem one flesh above another,**
    C or one man shall not **think himself above another;**
  B therefore **I say** unto you
A it is **not expedient that ye should have a king.** (23:7)

MOSIAH 24:14–15—
THE LORD PROMISES TO EASE BURDENS

A And I will also **ease** the **burdens**
  B which are **put upon your shoulders,**
    C that even **you cannot feel them upon your backs,**
      D even while you are **in bondage;**
        E and this **will I do**
          F that **ye may stand as witnesses** for me hereafter,
          F and that **ye may know** of a surety
        E that **I, the Lord God, do** visit
      D my people **in their afflictions.** (24:14)
    C And now it came to pass that the **burdens** which were laid
    upon Alma and his brethren were **made light;**
  B yea, the Lord did strengthen them that **they could bear up**
A their **burdens** with **ease,** (24:15)

MOSIAH 24:21—
GOD DELIVERS HIS PEOPLE FROM BONDAGE

A [God] eased their burdens, and had **delivered them**
  B out of **bondage;**
  B for they were in **bondage,**
A and none could **deliver them** (24:21)

MOSIAH 27:34—
THE NAMES OF MOSIAH'S SONS

A And four of them were the **sons of Mosiah**;
  B and their names were **Ammon, and Aaron,**
  B and **Omner, and Himni**;
A these were the names of the **sons of Mosiah**. (27:34)

MOSIAH 29:20—
GOD DELIVERS THE HUMBLE FROM BONDAGE

A But behold, **he did deliver them**
  B because they did **humble themselves before him**;
  B and because they **cried mightily unto him**
A **he did deliver them** out of bondage; (29:20)

Alma

ALMA 1:1—
KING MOSIAH ESTABLISHED LAWS

A nevertheless **he had established laws,**
  B and they were **acknowledged by the people;**
  B therefore **they were obliged to abide**
A by the **laws which he had made.** (1:1)

ALMA 2:22—
WATCHING THE CAMP OF THE AMLICITES

A Now those whom he had sent out to **watch the camp of the Amlicites**
  B were called **Zeram, and Amnor, and Manti, and Limher;**
  B **these were they** who went out with their men
A to **watch the camp of the Amlicites.** (2:22)

ALMA 3:6–7—
A CURSE FOR REBELLION

A And the skins of the **Lamanites** were dark,
  B according to the **mark** which was set upon their fathers,
    C which was a **curse** upon them
      D because of their transgression and their rebellion against their **brethren,**
        E who consisted of **Nephi, Jacob, and Joseph, and Sam,**

       E who were **just and holy men**. (3:6)
      D And their **brethren** sought to destroy them,
    C therefore they were **cursed**;
  B and the Lord God set a **mark** upon them,
A yea, upon **Laman and Lemuel**, (3:7)

ALMA 5:7–9—
BEING SAVED FROM DEATH AND HELL

Behold, he changed their hearts; yea, he awakened them out of a deep sleep, and they awoke unto God.

A Behold, **they were in the midst of darkness**; nevertheless,
  B **their souls** were illuminated by the light of the everlasting word;
    C yea, **they were encircled about**
      D by the **bands of death**, and the **chains of hell**, and an everlasting destruction did await them. (5:7)
        E And now **I ask of you**, my brethren, **were they destroyed**?
        E Behold, **I say unto you**, **Nay**, they were not. (5:8)
      D And again I ask, were the **bands of death** broken, and the **chains of hell**
    C which **encircled them about**, were they loosed? I say unto you,
  B Yea, they were loosed, and **their souls** did expand, and they did sing redeeming love.
A And I say unto you that **they are saved**. (5:9)

ALMA 5:11—
ALMA BELIEVES ABINADI

Behold, I can tell you—
  A did not **my father Alma believe** in the **words**
    B which were **delivered by** the mouth of **Abinadi**?
      C And was he not a **holy prophet**?
    B **Did he not speak the words** of God,
  A and my **father Alma believe them**? (5:11)

Alma 5:20–25—
Garments Must Be Purified and Washed

A I say unto you, can ye think of being saved when you have yielded yourselves to become **subjects to the devil**? (5:20)

  B I say unto you, ye will know at that day that **ye cannot be saved**;

    C for there can no man be saved except his **garments are washed white**; yea, his **garments must be purified** until they are **cleansed** from all stain,

      D through the blood of him of whom it has been spoken by **our fathers**, who should come to redeem his people from their sins. (5:21)

        E And now I ask of you, my brethren, how will any of you feel, if ye shall stand before the bar of God, having your garments stained with blood and **all manner of filthiness**?

          F Behold, what **will these things testify** against you? (5:22)

          F Behold **will they** not **testify** that ye are murderers,

        E yea, and also that ye are guilty of **all manner of wickedness**? (5:23)

      D Behold, my brethren, do ye suppose that such an one can have a place to sit down in the kingdom of God, with **Abraham**, with **Isaac**, and with **Jacob**, and also all the holy **prophets**,

    C whose **garments are cleansed and are spotless, pure and white**? (5:24)

  B I say unto you, Nay; except ye make our Creator a liar from the beginning, or suppose that he is a liar from the beginning, **ye cannot suppose that such can have place in the kingdom of heaven**;

A but they shall be cast out for they are the **children** of the kingdom **of the devil**. (5:25)

Alma 5:44–49—
How to Know Truth

A For **I am called** to speak after this manner, **according to the holy order of God**,

  B which is in **Christ Jesus**; yea, I am commanded to stand and testify unto this people the things which have been spoken by our fathers concerning the things **which are to come**. (5:44)

  C And this is not all. Do ye not suppose that I know of these things myself? Behold, I testify unto you that **I do know that these things whereof I have spoken are true**. And how do ye suppose that I know of their surety? (5:45)

    D Behold, I say unto you they are **made known unto me by the Holy Spirit of God**

      E Behold, I have fasted and prayed many days that **I might know these things of myself.**

      E And now **I do know of myself** that they are true;

    D for the Lord God hath **made them manifest unto me by his Holy Spirit**; and this is the spirit of revelation which is in me. (5:46)

  C And moreover, I say unto you that **it has thus been revealed unto me**, **that the words** which have been spoken by our fathers **are true**, even so according to the spirit of prophecy which is in me, which is also by the manifestation of the Spirit of God. (5:47) I say unto you, that I know of myself that whatsoever I shall say unto you, concerning that which is to come, is true;

 B and I say unto you, that I know that **Jesus Christ shall come**, yea, the Son, the Only Begotten of the Father, full of grace, and mercy, and truth. And behold, it is he that cometh to take away the sins of the world, yea, the sins of every man who steadfastly believeth on his name. (5:48)

A And now I say unto you that this is **the order after which I am called** . . . (5:49)

ALMA 5:62—
SPEAKING BY COMMAND AND INVITATION

A **I speak** by way of command unto you

 B that **belong to the church**;

 B and unto those who do not **belong to the church**

A **I speak** by way of invitation, (5:62)

ALMA 6:5—
HEARING THE WORD OF GOD

A Now I would that ye should understand that the **word of God**
    B was liberal **unto all**,
    B that **none were deprived** of the privilege of assembling
    themselves together
A to hear the **word of God**. (6:5)

ALMA 7:11–13—
JESUS CHRIST TAKES UPON HIMSELF OUR SINS AND PAINS

A And he shall go forth, suffering pains and afflictions and **temptations**
of every kind;
    B and this that the word might be fulfilled which saith he will **take
    upon him** the pains and the sicknesses of his people. (7:11)
        C And he will take upon him **death**, that he may loose the bands
        of death which bind his people;
            D and he will take upon him **their infirmities**,
                E that his bowels may be filled with **mercy**,
                    F **according to the flesh**,
                    F that he may know **according to the flesh**
                E how **to succor** his people
            D according to **their infirmities**. (7:12) Now the Spirit
            knoweth all things;
        C nevertheless the Son of God **suffereth** according to the flesh
    B that he might **take upon him** the sins of his people,
A that he might blot out their **transgressions** according to the power
of his deliverance; and now behold, this is the testimony which is in me.
(7:13)

ALMA 7:14–15—
WE MUST BE BORN AGAIN AND BE BAPTIZED

A Now I say unto you that ye must repent, and **be born again**; for the
Spirit saith if ye are not born again ye cannot inherit the kingdom of
heaven;
    B therefore **come** and be baptized unto repentance,

C that ye may be **washed from your sins,**

    D that ye may have faith on the Lamb of God, **who taketh away the sins** of the world,

    D who is mighty to save and to cleanse from all unrighteousness. (7:14)

C Yea, I say unto you come and fear not, and **lay aside every sin**, which easily doth beset you, which doth bind you down to destruction,

  B yea, **come** and go forth, and show unto your God that ye are willing to repent of your sins

A and enter into a covenant with him to keep his commandments, and witness it unto him this day by going into the **waters of baptism**. (7:15)

ALMA 8:4—
TEACHING PEOPLE IN THE LAND OF MELEK

A And he began to **teach the people** in the **land of Melek**

  B according to the **holy order of God,**

  B by **which he had been called;**

A and he began to **teach the people** throughout all the **land of Melek.** (8:4)

ALMA 9:12—
GOD'S JUDGMENTS

A yea, **he will visit you**

  B in **his anger,**

  B and in **his** fierce **anger**

A he will not turn away. (9:12)

ALMA 9:31–32—
HARD-HEARTED PEOPLE

Now it came to pass that when I, Alma, had spoken these words, behold,

  A the **people were wroth** with me

    B because **I said unto them that they were a hard-hearted and a stiffnecked people.** (9:31)

B And also because **I said unto them that they were a lost and a fallen people**

A **they were angry** with me, (9:32)

ALMA 10:6—
THOSE WITH HARD HEARTS CANNOT HEAR

A Nevertheless, I did harden **my heart,**

  B for I was called many times and **I would not hear;**

    C therefore **I knew** concerning these things,

    C yet **I would not know;**

  B therefore **I went on rebelling** against God,

A in the wickedness of **my heart,** (10:6)

ALMA 10:9—
THE HOLY MAN

A And the **angel said** unto me

  B **he is a holy man;**

  B wherefore I know **he is a holy man**

A because it was **said by an angel** of God. (10:9)

ALMA 11:40—
WHO RECEIVES ETERNAL LIFE?

A and **these are they**

  B that shall have **eternal life,**

  B and **salvation**

A cometh to **none else.** (11:40)

ALMA 12:11–17—
THE MEANING OF THE CHAINS OF HELL

And they that will harden their hearts, to them is given the lesser portion of the word until they know nothing concerning his mysteries;

A and then they are taken **captive by the devil**, and led by **his will down to destruction**.

  B Now this is what is meant by the **chains** of hell. (12:11)

    C And Amulek hath spoken plainly concerning **death**, and being raised from this mortality to a state of immortality,

      D and **being brought before** the bar of **God**, to be **judged** according to our works. (12:12)

      a Then if our **hearts**

       b have been **hardened**,

       b yea, if we have **hardened**

      a our **hearts** against the word, insomuch that it has not been found in us,

      E then will our **state be awful**, for then we shall be condemned. (12:13)

       F For our **words will condemn us**,

       F yea, all our **works will condemn us**; we shall not be found spotless;

       F and our **thoughts will also condemn us**;

      E and in this **awful state** we shall not dare to look up to our God; and we would fain be glad if we could command the rocks and the mountains to fall upon us to hide us from his presence. (12:14)

      D But this cannot be; we must come forth and **stand before him** in his glory, and in his power, and in his might, majesty, and dominion, and acknowledge to our everlasting shame that all his **judgments** are just; that he is **just** in all his works, and that he is merciful unto the children of men, and that he has all power to save every man that believeth on his name and bringeth forth fruit meet for repentance. (12:15)

    C And now behold, I say unto you then cometh a **death**, even a second **death**, which is a spiritual **death**; then is a time that whosoever **dieth** in his sins, as to a temporal **death**, shall also **die** a spiritual **death**; yea, he shall **die** as to things pertaining unto righteousness. (12:16)

  B Then is the time when their torments shall be as a lake of fire and brimstone, whose flame ascendeth up forever and ever; and then is the time that they shall be **chained**

A **down to an everlasting destruction**, according to the power and **captivity of Satan**, he having subjected them according to **his will**. (12:17)

ALMA 13:6–10—
TRUTHS REGARDING THE HIGH PRIESTHOOD

A And thus being **called** by this holy **calling**, and **ordained** unto the **high priesthood** of the holy **order** of **God**, to teach his commandments unto the children of men, that they also might enter into his rest— (13:6)
> B a This **high priesthood**
>> b being after the **order of his Son**, which **order** was from the foundation of the world; or in other words,
>>> c being **without beginning of days or end of years**, being prepared from eternity to all eternity, according to his foreknowledge of all things— (13:7)
>> C Now they were ordained after this manner—
>>> a being **called** with a holy **calling**,
>>>> b and ordained with a holy **ordinance**,
>>>>> c and taking upon them the **high priesthood** of the holy **order**,
>>> C a which **calling**,
>>>> b and **ordinance**,
>>>>> c and **high priesthood**, is without beginning or end— (13:8)
> B a Thus they become **high priests** forever,
>> b after the **order of the Son**, the Only Begotten of the Father,
>>> c who is **without beginning of days or end of years**, who is full of grace, equity, and truth. And thus it is. Amen. (13:9)

A Now, as I said concerning the holy **order**, or this **high priesthood**, there were many who were **ordained** and became high priests of **God**; (13:10)

ALMA 14:2–3—
ALMA AND AMULEK TESTIFY PLAINLY

A But the more part of them were desirous that **they might destroy Alma and Amulek;**
> B a for **they were angry with Alma,**
>> b because of the **plainness of his words** unto Zeezrom; and they also said that **Amulek** had lied unto them,
>> C and had reviled **against their law**
>> C and also **against their lawyers** and judges. (14:2)

B **a** And **they were also angry with Alma and Amulek**;

    b and because they had **testified so plainly** against their
    wickedness,

A **they sought to put them away** privily. (14:3)

ALMA 14:29—
PEOPLE FLEE FROM ALMA AND AMULEK

[T]hey were struck with great fear,

  A and **fled** from the presence of **Alma and Amulek**

    B even as a **goat** fleeth

    B with her young from **two lions**;

  A and thus they did **flee** from the presence of **Alma and Amulek**.
(14:29)

ALMA 15:3—
ZEEZROM'S WICKEDNESS

A And also Zeezrom lay sick at Sidom, with a **burning fever**,

  B which was caused by the **great tribulations** of his mind

    C on account of **his wickedness**,

      D for **he supposed that Alma and Amulek were no more**;

      D and **he supposed that they had been slain**

    C because of **his iniquity**.

  B And this great sin, and his **many other sins**,

A did harrow up his **mind until it did become exceedingly sore**,
(15:3)

ALMA 16:1—
PEACE IN THE LAND OF ZARAHEMLA

A And it came to pass in the **eleventh year** of the reign of the judges
over the people of Nephi,

  B on the **fifth day** of the **second month**,

    C there having been much **peace** in the land of Zarahemla,

    C there having been **no wars nor contentions** for a certain
    number of years,

B even until the **fifth day** of the **second month**
A in the **eleventh year**, (16:1)

ALMA 17:37–38—
MEN UNSUCCESSFULLY ATTEMPT TO SMITE AMMON

A But behold, every man that **lifted** his club to smite Ammon,
  B **he smote off their arms** with his sword;
    C for he did withstand their blows by smiting their arms with the edge of **his sword**, insomuch that they began to be astonished,
      D and began to **flee** before him;
        E yea, and they were **not few in number**;
      D and he caused them to **flee** by the strength of his arm. (17:37)
    C Now six of them had fallen by the sling, but he slew none save it were their leader with **his sword**;
  B and **he smote off** as many of **their arms**
A as were **lifted** against him, and they were not a few.

ALMA 18:6—
MEN ARE SLAIN FOR SCATTERING FLOCKS

A For he had **slain** many of them
  B because their brethren had **scattered their flocks** at the place of water;
  B and thus, because they had had their **flocks scattered**
A they were **slain**. (18:6)

ALMA 18:12–14—
AMMON IS CALLED RABBANAH

A therefore he was about to **return out of his presence**. (18:12)
  B And one of the king's servants said unto him, **Rabbanah**,
    C which is, being interpreted, **powerful**
      D or great **king**,
      D considering their **kings**
    C to be **powerful**;

B and thus he said unto him: **Rabbanah**, the king desireth thee to
stay. (18:13)
A Therefore Ammon **turned himself unto the king**, (18:14)

ALMA 18:16—
AMMON DEFENDS THE KING'S SERVANTS

A Is it because thou hast heard that I defended thy **servants**
  B and thy **flocks**,
    C and **slew** seven of their brethren
      D **with the sling**
      D and **with the sword**,
    C and **smote** off the arms of others,
  B in order to defend thy **flocks**
A and thy **servants**; (18:16)

ALMA 18:38—
AMMON TEACHES KING LAMONI AND HIS SERVANTS

A And he also **rehearsed unto them**
  B concerning the **rebellions**
    C of **Laman and Lemuel**,
    C and the **sons of Ishmael**,
  B yea, all their **rebellions**
A did he **relate unto them**; (18:38)

ALMA 18:39—
AMMON INSTRUCTS LAMONI AND HIS SERVANTS

[H]e expounded unto them the plan of redemption, which was prepared from
the foundation of the world;
  A and he also **made known unto them**
    B concerning the coming of **Christ**,
    B and all the works of the **Lord**
  A did he **make known unto them**. (18:39)

ALMA 19:6–7—
LAMONI'S CLOUD OF DARKNESS IS DISPELLED

A Now, this was what **Ammon desired**,

   B for **he knew** that king Lamoni was under the **power of God**;

     C he knew that the **dark veil of unbelief** was being cast away from his mind,

       D and the **light** which did **light up his mind**,

         E which was the **light of the glory of God**,

         E which was a marvelous **light of his goodness**—

       D yea, this **light** had infused such joy **into his soul**,

     C the **cloud of darkness** having been dispelled,

   B and that the light of everlasting life was lit up in his soul, yea, **he knew** that this had overcome his natural frame, and he was **carried away in God**— (19:6)

A Therefore, what the queen desired of him was **his** only **desire**. (19:7)

ALMA 19:13—
LAMONI SEES THE REDEEMER

A For as sure as thou livest, behold, I have seen my **Redeemer**;

   B and he shall **come forth**,

   B and **be born** of a woman,

A and **he shall redeem** all mankind who believe on his name. (19:13)

ALMA 20:4—
AMMON TRAVELS TO THE LAND OF MIDDONI

A But behold, I will go with thee to **the land of Middoni**;

   B for **the king** of the land of Middoni,

   B whose name is **Antiomno**, is a friend unto me;

A therefore I go to **the land of Middoni**,

ALMA 20:10–13—
LAMONI MEETS WITH HIS FATHER

A And he also said: Whither art thou going with this **Nephite**, who is one of the **children of a liar**? (20:10)

  B And it came to pass that **Lamoni rehearsed unto him** whither he was going, for he feared to offend him. (20:11)

    C And he also told him all the cause of **his tarrying** in his own kingdom,

    C that **he did not go** unto his father to the feast which he had prepared. (20:12)

  B And now when **Lamoni had rehearsed unto him** all these things, behold, to his astonishment, his father was angry with him, and said:

A Lamoni, thou art going to deliver these **Nephites**, who are **sons of a liar**. (20:13)

ALMA 20:26–27—
THE KING IS GREATLY ASTONISHED BY AMMON

A And when he saw that Ammon had no **desire** to destroy him,

  B and when he also saw the great love he had for **his son Lamoni**,

    C he was **astonished exceedingly**, and said:

      D Because this is all that thou hast desired, that I would **release thy brethren**,

        E and suffer that my son Lamoni should **retain his kingdom**,

        E behold, I will grant unto you that my son may **retain his kingdom** from this time and forever; and I will govern him no more—(20:26)

      D And I will also grant unto thee that **thy brethren may be cast out of prison**, and thou and thy brethren may come unto me, in my kingdom; for I shall greatly desire to see thee.

    C For the king was **greatly astonished** at the words which he had spoken,

  B and also at the words which had been spoken by **his son Lamoni**,

A therefore he was **desirous** to learn them. (20:27)

ALMA 25:16—
THE LAW OF MOSES STRENGTHENS FAITH IN CHRIST

A Now they did not suppose that **salvation** came by the law of Moses;
   B but the law of Moses did serve to strengthen their **faith** in Christ;
   B and thus they did retain a hope through **faith**,
A unto eternal **salvation**, (25:16)

ALMA 26:29—
AMMON SPEAKS TO HIS BRETHREN

A And we have **entered** into their houses and **taught them**,
   B and **we have taught them** in their streets;
   B yea, and **we have taught them** upon their hills;
A and we have also **entered** into their temples and their synagogues and **taught them**; (26:29)

ALMA 27:22—
THE NEPHITES ESTABLISH JERSHON
AS A LAND OF INHERITANCE

And it came to pass that the voice of the people came, saying:
   A Behold, **we will give** up
     B the **land of Jershon**,
       C which is **on the east** by the sea, which joins the **land Bountiful**,
       C which is **on the south** of the **land Bountiful**;
     B and this **land Jershon** is the land
   A which **we will give** unto our brethren for an inheritance. (27:22)

ALMA 29:1–7—
ALMA EXPRESSES HIS DESIRES

A O that I were an **angel**, and could have the **wish** of mine heart, that I might go forth and speak with the trump of God, with a voice to shake the **earth**, and cry repentance unto every people! (29:1) Yea, I would declare unto every soul, as with the voice of thunder, repentance and the plan of redemption, that they should repent and come unto our God, that there might not be more sorrow upon all the face of the earth. (29:2)

> **B** But behold, I am a man, and do sin in my wish; for **I ought to be content with the things which the Lord hath allotted unto me**. (29:3)
>
>> **C** I ought not to harrow up in my desires, the firm decree of a just God, for I know that **he granteth unto men according to their desire**, whether it be unto **death or unto life**;
>>
>>> **D** yea, **I know** that he allotteth unto men, yea, decreeth unto them decrees which are unalterable, according to their wills, whether they be unto salvation or unto destruction. (29:4)
>>> **D** Yea, **and I know** that good and evil have come before all men; he that knoweth not good from evil is blameless; but he that knoweth good and evil,
>>
>> **C** to him it is given according to his desires, whether he desireth good or evil, **life or death**, joy or remorse of conscience. (29:5)
>
> **B** Now, seeing that I know these things, **why should I desire more than to perform the work to which I have been called**? (29:6)

A Why should I **desire** that I were an **angel**, that I could speak unto all the ends of the **earth**? (29:7)

Alma 29:9—
Alma Glories in the Lord's Commandments

A I know that which the **Lord hath commanded me**,
> **B** and **I glory** in it.
> **B** **I do not glory** of myself,

A but I glory in that which the **Lord hath commanded me**; (29:9)

Alma 29:9–10—
Alma's Glory Is to Help Bring People to Repentance

A yea, and this is my **glory**,
> **B** that perhaps **I** may be an instrument in the
>> **C** hands of **God** to **bring**
>>> **D** some soul to **repentance**; (29:9)

    E and this is my **joy**. And behold, when I see many
     D of **my brethren** truly **penitent**,
   C and **coming** to the **Lord** their God,
  B then is **my soul**
A **filled with joy**; (29:10)

ALMA 29:14–16—
JOY WHEN OTHERS SUCCEED

A But I do not joy in my own success alone, but my **joy is more full**
  B because of the **success of my brethren**, (29:14)
   C who have been up to the land of Nephi. Behold, **they have labored** exceedingly, and have **brought forth much** fruit; and how great shall be their reward! (29:15)
  B Now, when I think of the **success of these my brethren** my soul is carried away,
A even to the separation of it from the body, as it were, so **great is my joy**. (29:16)

ALMA 30:4–5—
CONTINUAL PEACE

A And thus the people did have **no disturbance**
  B in all the **sixteenth year of the reign of the judges** over the people of Nephi. (30:4)
  B And it came to pass that in the commencement of the **seventeenth year of the reign of the judges**,
A there was **continual peace**. (30:5)

ALMA 30:6–12—
AN ANTI-CHRIST PREACHES TO THE PEOPLE

A But it came to pass in the latter end of the seventeenth year, there came a man into the land of Zarahemla, and he was **Anti-Christ**, for he **began to preach unto the people** against the prophecies which had been spoken by the prophets, concerning the coming of **Christ**. (30:6)

B Now **there was no law against a man's belief**; for it was strictly contrary to the commands of God that there should be a law which should bring men on to **unequal grounds**. (30:7)

   C For thus saith the scripture: **Choose ye** this day, whom ye will serve. (30:8)

      D Now if a man desired to serve God, it was his privilege; or rather, if he believed in God it was his privilege to serve him; but if he did not believe in him there was no law to **punish** him. (30:9)

      D But if he murdered he was punished unto death; and if he robbed he was also punished; and if he stole he was also punished; and if he committed adultery he was also punished; yea, for all this wickedness they were **punished** (30:10)

   C For there was a law that **men should be judged** according to their crimes.

   B Nevertheless, **there was no law against a man's belief**; therefore, a man was punished only for the crimes which he had done; therefore all men were on **equal grounds**. (30:11)

A And this **Anti-Christ**, whose name was Korihor, (and the law could have no hold upon him) **began to preach unto the people** that there should be no **Christ**. (30:12)

ALMA 30:44—
"ALL THINGS DENOTE THERE IS A GOD"

The scriptures are laid before thee,

   A yea, and all things **denote there is a God**;

      B yea, even the **earth**, and all things that are upon the face of it, yea, and **its motion**,

      B yea, and also all the **planets which move** in their regular form

   A do **witness that there is a Supreme Creator**. (30:44)

ALMA 30:50-52—
KORIHOR IS STRUCK DUMB

Now when Alma had said these words,

   A Korihor **was struck dumb**, that **he could not have utterance**, according to the words of Alma. (30:50)

B And now when the chief judge saw this, he **put forth his hand** and wrote Korihor, saying:

> **C Art thou convinced** of the power of God?

>> **D** In whom did ye desire that Alma should **show forth his sign**?

>>> **E** Would ye that he should **afflict others**, to show unto thee a sign?

>> **D** Behold, he has **showed unto you a sign**;

> **C** and now **will ye dispute more**? (30:51)

B And Korihor **put forth his hand** and wrote, saying:

A I know that **I am dumb**, for **I cannot speak**; (30:52)

ALMA 31:17–23—
CONCERNING THE RAMEUMPTON, OR HOLY STAND

[F]or the which holiness, O God,

> **A we thank thee**; and **we also thank thee** that thou hast elected us, that we may not be led away after the foolish traditions of our brethren,

>> **B** which doth bind them down to a **belief** of Christ,

>>> **C** which doth **lead their hearts to wander** far from thee, our God. (31:17)

>>>> **D** And again we thank thee, O God, that we are a **chosen** and holy people. (31:18) Amen. Now it came to pass that after Alma and his brethren and his sons had heard these prayers, they were astonished beyond all measure. (31:19)

>>>>> **E** For behold, **every man** did go forth and offer up these **same prayers**. (31:19)

>>>>>> **F** Now the place was called by them **Rameumptom**,

>>>>>> **F** which, being interpreted, is the **holy stand**. (31:20)

>>>>> **E** Now, from this stand they did offer up, **every man**, the **selfsame prayer** unto God,

>>>> **D** thanking their God that they were **chosen** of him,

>>> **C** and that he did not **lead them away** after the tradition of their brethren, and that their **hearts** were not stolen away

>> **B** to **believe** in things to come, which they knew nothing about. (30:22)

> **A** Now, after the people had all **offered up thanks** after this manner, (31:23)

ALMA 31:31–33—
THE LORD PROVIDES US WITH COMFORT

O Lord, my heart is exceedingly sorrowful; wilt thou comfort my soul in
Christ.
    A O Lord, wilt thou grant unto me that I may have **strength**, that I may
suffer with patience these **afflictions** which shall come upon me,
because of the **iniquity** of this people. (31:31)
        B O Lord, wilt thou **comfort my soul**, and give unto me success,
            C and also my **fellow laborers** who are with me—
            C yea, **Ammon**, and **Aaron**, and **Omner**, and also **Amulek** and
Zeezrom and also my **two sons**—
        B yea, even all these wilt thou comfort, O Lord. Yea, wilt thou
comfort their souls in Christ. (31:32)
    A Wilt thou grant unto them that they may have **strength**, that they
may bear their **afflictions** which shall come upon them because of the
iniquities of this people. (31:33)

ALMA 32:1—
PREACHING GOD'S WORD IN THE
SYNAGOGUES, HOUSES, AND STREETS

And it came to pass that they did go forth,
    A and began to **preach the word** of God unto the people,
        B entering into **their synagogues**,
        B and into **their houses**;
    A yea, and even they did **preach the word** in their streets. (32:1)

ALMA 32:5—
DESPISED BECAUSE OF THEIR POVERTY

And they came unto Alma; and the one who was the foremost among them
said unto him:
    A Behold, **what shall these my brethren do**,
        B for they are despised of all men because of their **poverty**, yea, and
more especially by **our priests**;
            C for they have cast us out of our **synagogues**

C which we have labored abundantly to build with our own
hands;
B and they have cast us out because of our exceeding **poverty**; and
we have no place to worship **our God**;
A and behold, **what shall we do?** (32:5)

ALMA 32:9–10—
WORSHIPPING GOD IN SYNAGOGUES ONLY?

Behold thy brother hath said, What shall we do?—
A for we are cast out of our **synagogues**,
B that we **cannot worship our God** (32:9)
C Behold **I say** unto you,
B do ye suppose that ye **cannot worship God**
A save it be in your **synagogues** only? (39:10)

ALMA 33:11—
RECEIVING MERCY BECAUSE OF THE SON

And thou didst hear me because of mine afflictions and my sincerity;
A and it is **because of thy Son**
B that **thou hast been thus merciful unto me**,
C therefore I will cry **unto thee** in all mine afflictions,
C for **in thee** is my joy;
B for **thou hast turned thy judgments away from me**,
A because of thy Son. (33:11)

ALMA 34:9—
THE GREAT SIGNIFICANCE OF THE ATONEMENT

A For **it is expedient** that an atonement should **be made**;
B for according to the great plan of the Eternal God there must be an
atonement made,
C or else all mankind must unavoidably **perish**;
D yea, **all are hardened**;
D yea, **all are fallen** and are lost,
C and must **perish**

B except it be through the **atonement**

A which **it is expedient** should **be made**. (34:9)

ALMA 34:10 —
JESUS CHRIST IS THE "GREAT AND LAST SACRIFICE"

A For it is expedient that there should be a **great and last sacrifice**;

    B yea, not a **sacrifice of man**,

        C neither of **beast**,

        C neither of any manner of **fowl**;

    B for it shall not be a **human sacrifice**;

A but it must be an **infinite and eternal sacrifice**. (34:10)

ALMA 34:13–14 —
THE GREAT AND LAST SACRIFICE

A Therefore, it is expedient that there should be a **great and last sacrifice**;

    B and then shall there be, or it is expedient there should be, a **stop to the shedding of blood**;

        C **then shall the law of Moses be fulfilled**;

            D yea, it shall be **all fulfilled**,

            D **every jot and tittle**,

        C and **none shall have passed away**. (34:13)

    B And behold, this is the **whole meaning of the law**,

A every whit pointing to that **great and last sacrifice**; (34:14)

ALMA 34:34 —
REPENTANCE DURING A CRISIS

A **Ye cannot say**, when ye are brought to that awful crisis,

    B that **I will repent**,

    B that **I will return** to my God.

A Nay, **ye cannot say** this; (34:34)

Alma 34:36—
The Lord Does Not Dwell in Unholy Temples

A And this I know, because the Lord hath said **he dwelleth not**

    B in **unholy temples,**

    B but in the **hearts of the righteous**

A doth **he dwell**; (34:36)

Alma 35:15—
Alma Grieves because of the People's Iniquity

A Now Alma, being **grieved**

    B for the **iniquity of his people**, yea for the wars, and the blood-
sheds, and the contentions

        C which were **among them;**

            D and having been to **declare the word,**

            D or sent to **declare the word,**

        C **among all the people** in every city;

    B and seeing that the hearts of the **people began to wax hard**, and
that they began to be offended because of the strictness of the word,

A his heart was exceedingly **sorrowful**. (35:15)

Alma 36:1–30—
Jesus Christ Removes Our Exquisite Pains

A My son, give ear to **my words;**

    B for I swear unto you, that **inasmuch as ye shall keep the
commandments of God ye shall prosper in the land** (36:1)

        C I would that ye should do **as I have done, in remembering
the captivity of our fathers;**

            D for they were **in bondage**, and none could **deliver them**
except it was the God of Abraham, and the God of Isaac, and
the God of Jacob; and he surely did **deliver them** in their
afflictions. (36:2) And now, O my son Helaman, behold, thou
art in thy youth, and therefore, I beseech of thee that thou wilt
hear my words and learn of me;

                E for I do know that whosoever shall put their **trust in God**
shall be **supported** in their **trials**, and their **troubles**, and

their **afflictions**, and **shall be lifted up at the last day**. (36:3)

F And I would not that ye think that I **know** of myself— not of the temporal but of the spiritual, not of the carnal mind but **of God** (36:4)

G Now, behold, I say unto you, if I had not been **born of God** I should not have known these things; but God has, by the mouth of his holy angel, made these things known unto me, not of any worthiness of myself. (36:5)

H For I went about with the sons of Mosiah, seeking to destroy the church of God; but behold, God sent his holy angel to stop us by the way. (36:6) And behold, he spake unto us, as it were the voice of thunder, and the whole earth did tremble beneath our **feet**; and we all **fell to the earth**, for the fear of the Lord came upon us. (36:7) But behold, the voice said unto me: Arise. And I arose and stood up, and beheld the angel. (36:8) And he said unto me: If thou wilt of thyself be destroyed, *seek no more to destroy the church of God.* (36:9) And it came to pass that I fell to the earth; and it was for the space of three days and three nights that I could not open my mouth, neither had I the use of **my limbs**. (36:10) And the angel spake more things unto me, which were heard by my brethren, but I did not hear them; for when I heard the words—If thou wilt be destroyed of thyself, *seek no more to destroy the church of God—* I was struck with such great fear and amazement lest perhaps I should be destroyed, that **I fell to the earth** and I did hear no more. (36:11)

I But I was **racked** with eternal **torment**, for my soul was **harrowed up** to the greatest degree and **racked** with **all my sins**. (36:12) Yea, I did remember **all my sins** and iniquities, for which I was **tormented** with the **pains of** hell; yea, I saw that I had rebelled against my God, and that I had not kept his holy commandments. (36:13) Yea, and I had murdered many of his children, or rather led them away unto destruction; yea, and in fine so great had been my iniquities, that the very thought of coming into the **presence of my God** did rack my soul with inexpressible horror. (36:14) Oh, thought I, that I could be banished and become extinct both soul and body, that I might not be brought to stand in the **presence of my God**, to be judged of my deeds. (36:15) And now, for three days and for three nights was I **racked**, even with the **pains of** a damned soul. (36:16)

    J And it came to pass that as I was thus **racked with torment**, while I was **harrowed up by the memory of my many sins**,

        K behold, I remembered also to have heard my father prophesy unto the people concerning the coming of one **Jesus Christ**, **a Son of God**, to atone for the sins of the world. (36:17)

        K Now, as my mind caught hold upon this thought, I cried within my heart: O **Jesus**, **thou Son of God**, have mercy on me, who am in the gall of bitterness, and am encircled about by the everlasting chains of death. (36:18)

    J And now, behold, when I thought this, I could remember my **pains no more**; yea, I was **harrowed up by the memory of my sins no more**. (36:19)

I And oh, what **joy**, and what marvelous light I did behold; yea, my soul was filled with **joy** as exceeding as was my **pain**! (36:20) Yea, **I say unto you**, my son, that there could be **nothing so exquisite** and so bitter as were **my pains**. Yea, and again **I say unto you**, my son, that on the other hand, there can be **nothing so exquisite** and sweet as was **my joy**. (36:21) Yea, methought **I saw**, even as our father Lehi saw, **God** sitting upon his throne, surrounded with numberless concourses of angels, in the attitude of singing and praising their God; yea, and my soul did long to be there. (36:22)

H But behold, my **limbs** did receive their strength again, and I **stood upon my feet**, and did manifest unto the people that I had been **born of God** (36:23) Yea, and from that time even until now, I have labored without ceasing,

G that I might bring souls unto repentance; that I might bring them to taste of the exceeding joy of which I did taste; that they might also be **born of God**, and be filled with the Holy Ghost. (36:24) Yea, and now behold, O my son, the Lord doth give me exceedingly great joy in the fruit of my labors; (36:26) For because of the word which he has imparted unto me, behold, many have been **born of God**, and have tasted as I have tasted, and have seen eye to eye as I have seen;

F therefore they do **know** of these things of which I have spoken, as I do **know**; and the **knowledge** which I have is **of God** (36:26)

E And I have been **supported** under **trials** and **troubles** of every kind, yea, and in all manner of **afflictions**; yea, **God has delivered** me from prison, and from bonds, and from death; yea, and I do put my **trust in him**, and he will still **deliver** me. (36:27) And I know that he will **raise me up at the last day**, to dwell with him in glory;

D yea, and I will praise him forever, for he has **brought our fathers out** of Egypt, and he has swallowed up the Egyptians in the Red Sea; and he **led them** by his power **into the promised land**; yea, and he has **delivered them out of bondage and captivity** from time to time. (36:28) Yea, and he has also **brought our fathers out** of the land of Jerusalem; and he has also, by his everlasting power, **delivered them out of bondage** and **captivity**, from time to time even down to the present day;

C and I have always **retained in remembrance their captivity**; yea, and ye also ought to **retain in remembrance, as I have done, their captivity**. (36:29)

B But behold, my son, this is not all; for ye ought to know as I do know, that **inasmuch as ye shall keep the commandments of God ye shall prosper in the land**; and ye ought to know also, that inasmuch as ye will not keep the commandments of God ye shall be cut off from his presence.

A Now this is according to **his word** (36:30)

ALMA 37:1–13—
THE LORD USES SMALL MEANS TO CONFOUND THE WISE

A And now, **my son Helaman**, I **command** you that ye take the records which have been entrusted with me; (37:1) And I also **command** you that ye keep a record of this people,= according as I have done,

    B upon the plates of Nephi, and keep all these things sacred which I have kept, even as I have kept them; for it is **for a wise purpose that they are kept**. (37:2) And these plates of brass, which contain these engravings, which have the records of the holy scriptures upon them, which have the genealogy of our forefathers, even from the beginning— (37:3)

        C Behold, it has been prophesied by our fathers, that they should be kept and handed down from one generation to another, and be kept and preserved by the hand of the Lord until they should **go forth unto every nation, kindred, tongue, and people**, that **they shall know of the mysteries** contained thereon. (37:4)

            D And now behold, if **they** are kept they must retain their brightness; yea, and **they** will retain their brightness; yea, and also shall all the **plates** which do contain that which is **holy writ**. (37:5)

                E Now ye may suppose that this is foolishness in me; but behold I say unto you, that by **small and simple things** are great things brought to pass; and **small means** in many instances doth **confound the wise**. (37:6)

                    F And the Lord God doth work by means to bring about his **great and eternal purposes**;

                E and by very **small means** the Lord doth **confound the wise** and bringeth about the salvation of many souls. (37:7)

            D And now, it has hitherto been wisdom in God that **these things** should be preserved; for behold, they have enlarged the memory of this people, yea, and convinced many of the error of their ways, and brought them to the knowledge of their God unto the salvation of their souls. (37:8) Yea, I say unto you, were it not for **these things** that these **records** do contain, which are on these **plates**, Ammon and his brethren could not have convinced so many thousands of the Lamanites of the incorrect tradition of their fathers; yea, these **records** and their **words** brought them unto repentance; that is, they brought them to the knowledge of the Lord their God, and to rejoice in Jesus Christ their Redeemer. (37:9)

C And who knoweth but what they will be **the means of bringing many thousands of them**, yea, and also many thousands of our stiffnecked brethren, the Nephites, who are now hardening their hearts in sin and iniquities, to the knowledge of their Redeemer? (37:10) Now these **mysteries are not yet fully made known** unto me; therefore I shall forbear. (37:11)

B And it may suffice if I only say **they are preserved for a wise purpose**, which purpose is known unto God; for he doth counsel in wisdom over all his works, and his paths are straight, and his course is one eternal round. (37:12)

A O remember, remember, **my son Helaman**, how strict are the **commandments** of God. (37:13)

ALMA 37:21–26—
CONCERNING THE INTERPRETERS

A And now, I will speak unto you concerning those twenty-four plates, that ye keep them, that the mysteries and the works of darkness, and their secret works, or the **secret works** of those people who have been destroyed, may be made **manifest unto this people**;

B yea, all their **murders**, and **robbings**, and their **plunderings**, and all their **wickedness** and **abominations**,

C may be made manifest unto this people; yea, and that ye preserve **these interpreters**. (37:21)

D For behold, the Lord saw that his people began to **work in darkness**, yea, work **secret murders** and **abominations**; therefore the Lord said, if they did not repent they should be destroyed from off the face of the earth. (37:22) And the Lord said: I will prepare unto my servant Gazelem, a stone, which shall shine forth in darkness unto light,

E that **I may discover** unto my people who serve me,

      E that **I may discover** unto them the works of their
      brethren,
        D yea, their **secret works**, their **works of darkness**, and
        their **wickedness** and **abominations**. (37:23)
     C And now, my son, **these interpreters** were prepared that the
     word of God might be fulfilled, which he spake, saying: (37:24)
   B I will bring forth out of darkness unto light all their secret works
and their **abominations**; and except they repent I will destroy them
from off the face of the earth; and I will bring to light all their secrets
and **abominations**, unto every nation that shall hereafter possess the
land. (37:25) And now, my son, we see that they did not repent; therefore they have been destroyed,
A and thus far the word of God has been fulfilled; yea, their **secret
abominations** have been brought out of darkness and **made known
unto us**. (37:26)

ALMA 37:34 —
LEARN WISDOM WHEN YOUNG

A O, remember, my son, and **learn wisdom**
  B in **thy youth**;
  B yea, learn in **thy youth**
A to **keep the commandments** of God. (37:34)

ALMA 40:23 —
THE SOUL AND BODY ARE
RESTORED AT THE RESURRECTION

A The **soul** shall be restored
  B to the **body**,
  B and the **body**
A to the **soul**; (40:23)

Alma 41:10–12—
"Wickedness Never Was Happiness"

A Do not suppose, because it has been spoken concerning **restoration**, that ye shall be restored from sin to happiness.

  B Behold, I say unto you, **wickedness never was happiness**. (41:10)

    C And now, my son, all men that are in a **state of nature**,

      D or I would say, in a **carnal state**,

        E are in the **gall of bitterness**

        E and in the **bonds of iniquity**;

      D they are **without God** in the world,

    C and they have gone **contrary to the nature of God**;

  B therefore, they are in a **state contrary to the nature of happiness**. (41:11)

A And now behold, is the meaning of the word **restoration** to take a thing of a natural state and place it in an unnatural state, or to place it in a state opposite to its nature? (41:12)

Alma 42:5–8—
Cut Off from God's Presence

For behold, if Adam had put forth his hand immediately, and partaken of the tree of life, he would have lived forever, according to the word of God, having no space for repentance;

A yea, and also the word of God would have been void, and the **great plan** of salvation would have been **frustrated** (42:5)

  B But behold, it was appointed unto man **to die**—

    C therefore, as they were cut off from the **tree of life**

      D they should be **cut off from the face of the earth**—

        E and **man became lost** forever,

        E yea, they became **fallen man**. (42:6)

      D And now, ye see by this that our first parents were **cut off both temporally**

    C and spiritually from the **presence of the Lord**; and thus we see they became subjects to follow after their own will. (42:7)

  B Now behold, it was not expedient that man should be reclaimed from this **temporal death**,

A for that would **destroy the great plan** of happiness. (42:8)

ALMA 42:13—
JUSTICE, MERCY AND OUR PROBATIONARY STATE

A Therefore, according to **justice**,
  B the plan of redemption **could not be brought about**,
    C only on **conditions** of repentance of men
      D in this **probationary state**,
      D yea, this **preparatory state**;
    C for except it were for these **conditions**,
  B mercy **could not take effect**
A except it should destroy the work of **justice**. (42:13)

ALMA 42:14—
"THE GRASP OF JUSTICE"

A And thus we see that all mankind were **fallen**,
  B and they were in the grasp of **justice**;
  B yea, the **justice** of God,
A which consigned them forever to be **cut off from his presence**.
(42:14)

ALMA 42:15—
JESUS CHRIST'S ATONEMENT AND "THE PLAN OF MERCY"

A And now, the **plan of mercy** could not be brought about
  B except an **atonement should be made**;
  B therefore **God himself atoneth** for the sins of the world,
A to bring about the **plan of mercy**, (42:15)

ALMA 43:38—
NEPHITE SHIELDS

While on the other hand, there was now and then a man fell among the Nephites, by their swords and the loss of blood,
  A they being **shielded** from
    B the more **vital parts of the body**,

B or the more **vital parts of the body**
A being **shielded** from the strokes of the Lamanites,

ALMA 46:15—
CHRISTIANS ARE BELIEVERS IN CHRIST

And those who did belong to the church were faithful;
   A yea, all those who were true **believers in Christ** took upon them,
      B gladly, the **name of Christ**,
      B or **Christians as they were called**,
   A because of their **belief in Christ** who should come. (46:15)

ALMA 46:23–24—
SYMBOLISM OF JOSEPH'S RENT COAT

A yea, we are a **remnant** of the seed **of Joseph**,
   B whose **coat was rent by his brethren** into many pieces;
      C yea, and now behold, let us remember to **keep the commandments of God**,
   B or our **garments shall be rent by our brethren**, and we be cast into prison, or be sold, or be slain. (46:23)
A Yea, let us preserve our liberty as a **remnant of Joseph**; (46:24)

ALMA 46:24—
JOSEPH'S GARMENT

A Even as this **remnant of garment** of my son hath been preserved,
   B so shall a **remnant of the seed** of my son be preserved
      C by the hand of **God**,
      C and be taken unto **himself**,
   B while the **remainder of the seed** of Joseph shall perish,
A even as the **remnant of his garment**. (46:24)

Alma 49:2-3—
Battling with Arrows and Stones

A And behold, the **city had been rebuilt**, and Moroni had stationed an army by the borders of the city, and they had cast up dirt around about to shield them
    B from the **arrows**
        C and the **stones**
            D of the **Lamanites**;
            D for behold, **they** fought
        C with **stones**
    B and with **arrows**. (49:2)
A Behold, I said that the **city** of Ammonihah **had been rebuilt**. (49:3)

Alma 49:18-19—
Regarding Nephite Fortifications

A Now behold, the **Lamanites** could not **get into their forts** of security by any other way
    B save it were by the **entrance**,
        C because of the **highness** of the bank which had been thrown up,
        C and the **depth** of the ditch which had been dug round about,
    B save it were by the **entrance**. (49:18)
A And thus were the **Nephites** prepared to destroy all such as should attempt to climb up to **enter the fort** by any other way, (49:19)

Alma 50:14—
The Cities of Moroni and Aaron

A And they also began a foundation for a **city** between
    B the city of **Moroni**
        C and the city of **Aaron**,
        C joining the borders of **Aaron**
    B and **Moroni**;
A and they called the name of the **city**, or the land, Nephihah. (50:14)

ALMA 52:3—
AMMORON WAS APPOINTED KING

A And it came to pass that the **brother of Amalickiah was appointed** king over the people;

    B and his name was **Ammoron**;

    B thus king **Ammoron**,

A the **brother of king Amalickiah, was appointed** to reign in his stead. (52:3)

ALMA 52:28–31—
THE ARMIES OF LEHI AND MORONI

And now behold, when the chief captains of the Lamanites had beheld Lehi with his army coming against them, they fled in much confusion, lest perhaps they should not obtain the city Mulek before Lehi should overtake them;

A for they were **wearied because of their march**,

    B and the **men of Lehi** were **fresh**. (52:28)

        C Now the Lamanites did not know that **Moroni** had been in their rear **with his army**; and all they feared was Lehi and his men. (52:29)

            D Now **Lehi** was not desirous to overtake them till they should meet **Moroni and his army**. (52:30)

                E And it came to pass that before the **Lamanites** had retreated far

            D they were surrounded by the **Nephites**,

        C by the **men of Moroni** on one hand,

    B and the **men of Lehi** on the other, all of whom were **fresh** and full of strength;

A but the Lamanites were **wearied because of their** long **march**. (52:31)

ALMA 53:1—
GUARDING THE LAMANITE PRISONERS

A And it came to pass that they did set **guards** over the prisoners of the Lamanites,

    B and did compel them to go forth and bury their **dead**,

B yea, and also the **dead** of the Nephites who were slain;
A and Moroni placed men over them to **guard** them while they should perform their labors. (53:1)

ALMA 53:8-9—
INTRIGUE AMONG SOME OF THE NEPHITES

And now it came to pass that the armies of the Lamanites, on the west sea, south, while in the absence of Moroni

  A on account of some **intrigue amongst the Nephites**,

    B which caused **dissensions**

      C amongst them,

        D had **gained some ground** over the Nephites,

        D yea, insomuch that they had **obtained possession** of a number of their cities in that part of the land. (53:8)

      C And thus because of iniquity **amongst themselves**,

    B yea, because of **dissensions**

  A and **intrigue among themselves** (53:9)

ALMA 54:12—
MORONI'S WORDS AGAINST AMMORON

  A I will **come against you**

    B with **my armies**;

    B yea, even I will arm **my women and my children**,

  A and I will **come against you**, (54:12)

ALMA 56:38—
ANTIPUS AND HIS ARMY

  A But behold, it was **night**;

    B therefore they did not **overtake** us,

    B neither did Antipus **overtake** them;

  A therefore we did camp for the **night**. (56:38)

ALMA 57:25–26—
GOD'S GOODNESS AND POWER

And it came to pass that there were two hundred, out of my two thousand and sixty, who had fainted because of the loss of blood;

   A nevertheless, according to the **goodness of God**,

      B and to our great **astonishment**, and also the joy of **our whole army**,

         C there was not **one soul** of them who did perish;

         C yea, and neither was there **one soul** among them who had not received many wounds. (57:25)

      B And now, their preservation was **astonishing** to **our whole army**, yea, that they should be spared while there was a thousand of our brethren who were slain.

   A And we do justly ascribe it to the **miraculous power of God**, (57:26)

ALMA 60:15–16—
UNRIGHTEOUS DESIRE FOR POWER

For were it not for the wickedness which first commenced at our head,

   A we could have **withstood our enemies** that they could have gained no power over us. (60:15)

      B Yea, **had it not been for** the war which broke out among ourselves;

         C yea, were it not for these king-men, who caused **so much bloodshed among ourselves**;

            D yea, at the time we were **contending among ourselves**,

               E if we had **united** our strength as we hitherto have done;

                  F yea, had it not been for the **desire of power and authority** which those king-men had over us;

                  F had they been **true to the cause of our freedom**,

               E and **united** with us,

            D and gone forth against our enemies, instead of taking up **their swords against us**,

         C which was the cause of **so much bloodshed among ourselves**;

      B yea, **if we had** gone forth against them in the strength of the Lord,

   A we should have **dispersed our enemies**, (60:16)

ALMA 60:22—
SITTING IN IDLENESS

A Yea, will ye **sit in idleness**
   B while ye are surrounded with **thousands** of those,
   B yea, and **tens of thousands**,
A who do also **sit in idleness**, (60:22)

ALMA 61:12–13—
THE YOKE OF BONDAGE

A We would **subject ourselves** to the yoke of bondage
   B if it were requisite with the justice of God, or if he should **command us** so to do. (61:12)
   B But behold he doth not **command us**
A that we shall **subject ourselves** to our enemies, (61:13)

ALMA 63:11–13—
SHIBLON GIVES THE ENGRAVINGS TO HELAMAN

A Therefore it became expedient for **Shiblon** to confer those sacred things, before **his death**,
   B upon the son of Helaman, who was called **Helaman**,
     C being **called after the name of his father**. (63:11)
       D Now behold, all **those engravings** which were in the possession of Helaman
         E were written and **sent forth** among the children of men throughout all the land,
         E save it were those parts which had been commanded by Alma should not **go forth**. (63:12)
       D Nevertheless, **these things** were to be kept sacred,
     C and handed down from **one generation to another**;
   B therefore, in this year, they had been conferred upon **Helaman**,
A before the **death of Shiblon**. (63:13)

Helaman

HELAMAN 1:3-4—
CONTENDING FOR THE JUDGMENT-SEAT

A Now these are their names who did **contend for the judgment-seat**, who did also **cause the people to contend:**
    B **Pahoran, Paanchi, and Pacumeni.** (1:3)
    B Now these are not all the **sons of Pahoran,** (for he had many)
A but these are they who did **contend for the judgment-seat**; therefore, they did **cause** three **divisions among the people.** (1:4)

HELAMAN 2:1-2—
HELAMAN WAS APPOINTED TO THE JUDGMENT-SEAT

A therefore there began to be a contention again among **the people**
    B concerning who should **fill the judgment-seat.** (2:1)
        C And it came to pass that **Helaman,**
        C who was the son of **Helaman,**
    B was appointed to **fill the judgment-seat,**
A by the voice of **the people.** (2:2)

HELAMAN 3:24-26—
THOUSANDS JOIN THE CHURCH

And it came to pass that in this same year there was exceedingly great prosperity in the church,

A insomuch that there were **thousands**

    B who did **join themselves unto the church**

        C and were **baptized** unto repentance.

            D And so great was the **prosperity** of the church, and so many the blessings which were poured out upon the people,

                E that even the **high priests**

                E and the **teachers** were themselves astonished beyond measure.

            D And it came to pass that the work of the Lord did **prosper**

        C unto the **baptizing**

    B and **uniting to the church** of God, many souls,

A yea, even tens of **thousands**.

HELAMAN 4:9–19—
BOASTING IN OUR OWN STRENGTH

A And it came to pass in the sixtieth year of the reign of the judges, **Moronihah did succeed with his armies in obtaining many parts of the land**;

    B yea, they regained many **cities** which had fallen into the hands **of the Lamanites**. (4:9)

        C And it came to pass in the **sixty and first year of the reign of the judges**

            D they succeeded in **regaining even the half of all their possessions**. (4:10)

                E Now this **great loss** of the Nephites, and the **great slaughter** which was among them, **would not have happened had it not been for their wickedness** and their abomination which was among them; yea, and it was among those also who professed to belong to the church of God. (4:11)

                    F And it was because of the **pride** of their hearts, because of their exceeding riches, yea, it was because of their **oppression to the poor, withholding their food** from the hungry, **withholding their clothing** from the naked, and **smiting their humble brethren** upon the cheek, making a **mock of that which was sacred**, **denying the spirit of prophecy** and of revelation, **murdering, plundering, lying, stealing**, committing

adultery, rising up in great **contentions**,

     G and deserting away into the **land** of Nephi,

       H among the **Lamanites**— (4:12)

         I And because of this their great wickedness, and their boastings in their **own strength**,

         I they were left in their **own strength**;

       H therefore they did not prosper, but were afflicted and smitten, and driven before the **Lamanites**,

     G until they had lost possession of almost all their **lands**. (4:13)

   F But behold, Moronihah did preach many things unto the people because of **their iniquity**, and also Nephi and Lehi, who were the sons of Helaman, did preach many things unto the people, (yea, and did prophesy many things unto them concerning **their iniquities**, and what should come unto them if they did not repent of **their sins**. (4:14)

  E And it came to pass that they did repent, and inasmuch **as they did repent they did begin to prosper**. (4:15)

 D For when Moronihah saw that they did repent he did venture to lead them forth from place to place, and from city to city, even until they had **regained the one-half of their property and the one-half of all their lands**. (4:16)

  C And thus ended the **sixty and first year of the reign of the judges**. (4:17)

 B And it came to pass in the sixty and second year of the reign of the judges, that Moronihah could obtain no more **possessions over the Lamanites**. (4:18)

A Therefore they did abandon their design to obtain the remainder of their lands, for so numerous were the Lamanites that it became impossible for the Nephites to obtain more power over them; therefore **Moronihah did employ all his armies in maintaining those parts which he had taken**. (4:19)

HELAMAN 5:48–50—
ANGELS DESCEND FROM HEAVEN AND MINISTER

A And now, when **they heard** this they cast up their eyes as if to behold from whence the voice came; and behold, **they saw** the heavens open;

B and angels came down out of heaven and **ministered unto them**. (5:48)

   C And there were about three hundred souls who saw and heard these things; and they were bidden to **go forth**

      D and **marvel not**,

      D **neither** should they **doubt**. (5:49)

   C And it came to pass that they did **go forth**,

  B and did **minister unto the people**,

A declaring throughout all the regions round about all the things which **they had heard and seen**, (5:50)

HELAMAN 6:7–13—
PEACE AND WEALTH IN THE LAND

A And behold, there was **peace** in all the land,

  B insomuch that the Nephites did go into **whatsoever part of the land they would**, whether among the Nephites or the Lamanites. (6:7) And it came to pass that the Lamanites did also go whithersoever they would, whether it were among the Lamanites or among the Nephites; and thus they did have free intercourse one with another, **to buy and to sell**, **and to get gain**, according to their desire. (6:8)

   C And it came to pass that they became exceedingly **rich**, both the Lamanites and the Nephites;

    D and they did have an exceeding **plenty** of **gold**, and of **silver**, and of **all manner** of **precious metals**, **both** in the **land** south and in the **land** north. (6:9)

     E Now the land **south**

      F was called **Lehi**

       G and the land **north**

        H was called **Mulek**,

         I which was after the son of **Zedekiah**;

         I for the **Lord**

        H did bring **Mulek**

       G into the land **north**,

      F and **Lehi**

     E into the land **south**. (6:10)

    D And behold, there was **all manner** of **gold** in **both these lands**, and of **silver**, and of **precious ore** of every kind;

   C and there were also curious workmen, who did work all kinds of ore and did refine it; and thus they did become **rich**. (6:11)

B They did raise grain in abundance, both **in the north and in the south**; and they did **flourish exceedingly**, both **in the north and in the south**. And they did multiply and wax exceedingly strong in the land. (6:12) And they did raise many flocks and herds, yea, many fatlings. Behold their women did toil and spin, and did make all manner of cloth, of fine-twined linen and cloth of every kind, to clothe their nakedness.

A And thus the sixty and fourth year did pass away in **peace**. (6:13)

HELAMAN 6:15—
DOUBLE MURDER ON THE JUDGMENT-SEAT

A And it came to pass that in the **sixty and sixth year** of the reign of the judges,

    B behold, **Cezoram was murdered**

        C by an unknown hand as **he**

            D sat upon the **judgment-seat**.

        C And it came to pass that in the same year, that **his son**,

    B who had been appointed by the people in his stead, **was also murdered**.

A And thus ended the **sixty and sixth year**. (6:15)

HELAMAN 6:21–26—
GADIANTON AND HIS BAND OF ROBBERS

A But behold, **Satan**

    B did stir up the **hearts** of the more part of the Nephites,

        C insomuch that they did unite with those **bands** of robbers,

            D and did enter into their **covenants** and their **oaths**,

                E that they would **protect and preserve one another** in whatsoever difficult circumstances they should be placed,

                    F that they should not suffer for their **murders**, and their **plunderings**, and their **stealings**. (6:21)

                        G And it came to pass that they did have their signs, yea, their **secret signs**, and their **secret words**;

                            H and this that they might distinguish a **brother** who had entered into the covenant,

> **H** that whatsoever wickedness his **brother** should do he should not be injured by his **brother**,
>> **G** nor by those who did belong to his band, who had taken this **covenant**. (6:22)
>>> **F** And thus they might **murder**, and **plunder**, and **steal**, and commit whoredoms and all manner of wickedness, contrary to the laws of their country and also the laws of their God. (6:23)
>>>> **E** And whosoever of those who belonged to their band should reveal unto the world of their wickedness and their abominations, **should be tried**, not according to the laws of their country, but **according to the laws of their wickedness**, which had been given by Gadianton and Kishkumen. (6:24)
>>>>> **D** Now behold, it is these secret **oaths** and **covenants** which Alma commanded his son should not go forth unto the world, lest they should be a means of bringing down the people unto destruction. (6:25) Now behold, those secret **oaths** and **covenants** did not come forth
>>>> **C** unto **Gadianton** from the records which were delivered unto Helaman;
>>> **B** but behold, they were put into the **heart** of Gadianton
>> **A** by that **same being** who did entice our first parents to partake of the forbidden fruit— (6:26)

HELAMAN 7: 1–3—
NEPHI PREACHES AND PROPHESIES

A Nephi, the son of Helaman, **returned to the land** of Zarahemla from the land northward. (7:1)
> **B** For he had been forth **among the people** who were in the land northward
>> **C** and **did preach** the word of God unto them,
>> **C** and **did prophesy** many things unto them; (7:2)
> **B** And they did reject all his words, insomuch that he could not stay **among them**,

A but **returned** again **unto the land** of his nativity. (7:3)

HELAMAN 7:6–9—
CONCERNING THOSE WHO ARE SLOW TO DO INIQUITY

A Now this great **iniquity had come upon the Nephites**, in the space of not many years;

    B and when Nephi saw it, his **heart was swollen with sorrow** within his breast;

        C and he did exclaim in the agony of his **soul**: (7:6)

            D Oh, that **I could have had my days in the days** when my father Nephi first came out of the land of Jerusalem, that I could have joyed with him in the promised land;

                E then were his **people easy to be entreated**,

                    F **firm to keep the commandments** of God,

                    F and **slow to be led to do iniquity**;

                E and **they were quick to hearken** unto the words of the Lord— (7:7)

            D Yea, if **my days could have been in those days**,

        C then would my **soul** have had joy in the righteousness of my brethren. (7:8)

    B But behold, I am consigned that these are my days, and that my **soul shall be filled with sorrow**

A because of this the **wickedness of my brethren**. (7:9)

HELAMAN 8:20—
THE PROPHET JEREMIAH TESTIFIES OF JERUSALEM'S DESTRUCTION

Jeremiah [testified of Christ],

    A (**Jeremiah** being that same prophet who **testified**

        B of the **destruction of Jerusalem**)

        B and now we know that **Jerusalem was destroyed**

    A according to the **words of Jeremiah**. (8:20)

HELAMAN 8:27—
THE JUDGE IS MURDERED

A yea, go ye in unto the **judgment-seat**,

    B and **search**;

    C and behold, your judge is **murdered**,

        D and **he lieth in his blood**;

    C and he hath been **murdered** by his brother,

  B who **seeketh**

A to sit in the **judgment-seat**. (8:27)

HELAMAN 10:4–5—
NEPHI WILL BE BLESSED FOREVER

A **Blessed art thou**, Nephi,

  B for those things which **thou hast done**; for I have beheld how thou hast with **unwearyingness** declared the word,

    C which **I have given** unto thee, unto this people.

      D And thou hast not feared them, and hast **not sought thine own life**,

      D but hast **sought my will**,

    C and to **keep my commandments**.

  B And now, because **thou hast done** this with such **unwearyingness**,

A behold, I will **bless thee** forever;

HELAMAN 10:7—
POWER TO SEAL ON EARTH AND IN HEAVEN

A Behold, I give unto you **power**,

  B that whatsoever ye shall seal on **earth** shall be sealed in **heaven**;

  B and whatsoever ye shall loose on **earth** shall be loosed in **heaven**;

A and thus shall ye have **power** among this people. (10:7)

HELAMAN 10:13–15—
THE PEOPLE HARDEN THEIR HEARTS

Now behold, notwithstanding that great miracle which Nephi had done in telling them concerning the death of the chief judge,

  A they did **harden their hearts** and did not **hearken** unto the words of the Lord. (10:13)

  B Therefore **Nephi did declare** unto them the word of the Lord, saying:

C Except ye repent, thus saith the Lord,

   C ye shall be smitten even unto destruction. (10:14)

 B And it came to pass that when **Nephi had declared** unto them the word,

A behold, they did still **harden their hearts** and would not **hearken** unto his words; (10:15)

HELAMAN 11:2 —
THE LENGTH OF THE WAR

A And this war **did last**

  B all that **year**;

  B and in the seventy and third **year**

A it **did** also **last**. (11:2)

HELAMAN 11:5–6 —
"THE WORK OF DESTRUCTION"

A And thus in the **seventy and fourth year** the famine did continue,

  B and the **work of destruction**

    C did cease by the **sword**

    C but became sore by **famine**. (11:5)

  B And this **work of destruction**

A did also continue in the **seventy and fifth year**. (11:6)

HELAMAN 11:21 —
PEACE DURING THE SEVENTY AND SEVENTH YEAR

A And the **seventy and seventh** year

  B began in **peace**;

    C and the **church** did spread throughout the face of all the land;

      D and the more part of the **people**,

      D both the **Nephites** and the **Lamanites**,

    C did belong to the **church**;

  B and they did have exceedingly great **peace** in the land;

A and thus ended the **seventy and seventh** year. (11:21)

Helaman 12:22–23—
Repent and Be Saved

A for this cause, that men might **be saved**,

  B hath **repentance** been declared. (12:22)

  B Therefore, blessed are they who will **repent** and hearken unto the voice of the Lord their God;

A for these are they that shall **be saved**. (12:23)

Helaman 13:5–9—
The Sword of Justice

And he said unto them: Behold, I, Samuel, a Lamanite, do speak the words of the Lord . . .

  A the **sword** of justice hangeth over this people;

    B and **four hundred years** pass not away save the sword of justice falleth upon this people. (13:5)

      C Yea, **heavy destruction** awaiteth this people, and it surely cometh unto this people,

        D and nothing can save this people **save it be repentance** and faith on the Lord Jesus Christ, who surely shall come into the world, and shall suffer many things and shall be slain for his people. (13:6)

          E And behold, an angel of the Lord hath **declared it** unto me, and he did bring **glad tidings** to my soul.

          E And behold, I was sent unto you to **declare it** unto you also, that ye might have **glad tidings**; but behold ye would not receive me. (13:7)

        D Therefore, thus saith the Lord: Because of the hardness of the hearts of the people of the Nephites, **except they repent**

      C I will **take away my word** from them, and I will **withdraw my Spirit** from them, and I will suffer them no longer, and I will turn the hearts of their brethren against them. (13:8)

    B And **four hundred years** shall not pass away before I will cause that they shall be smitten;

  A yea, I will visit them with the **sword** and with famine and with pestilence. (13:9)

HELAMAN 13:11—
RETURN UNTO THE LORD

A But if ye will **repent and return unto the Lord** your God I will turn away mine anger,

    B **saith the Lord**;

    B yea, thus **saith the Lord**,

A blessed are they who will **repent and turn unto me**, (13:11)

HELAMAN 13:20—
HIDING UP YOUR TREASURES

A And the day shall come that they shall **hide up their treasures**,

    B because they have set their **hearts upon riches**;

    B and because they have set their **hearts upon their riches**,

A I will **hide up their treasures** when they shall flee before their enemies; (13:20)

HELAMAN 13:24–25—
WO TO THOSE WHO CAST OUT THE PROPHETS

Yea, wo unto this people, because of this time which has arrived,

    A that ye do **cast out the prophets**, and do mock them,

        B and **cast stones** at them,

            C and do **slay them**, and do all manner of iniquity unto them,

                D even as **they did of old time**. (13:24)

                    E And now when **ye talk**,

                    E **ye say**:

                D If our days had been in the **days of our fathers of old**,

            C we would not have **slain the prophets**;

        B we would not **have stoned them**,

A and **cast them out**. (13:25)

Helaman 13:27—
Walking after Pride

A But behold, if a **man shall come** among you **and shall say**:

   B **Do this**, and there is no iniquity; **do that** and ye shall not suffer;

      C yea, he will say: **Walk after the pride** of your own hearts;

      C yea, **walk after the pride** of your eyes,

   B and **do whatsoever** your heart desireth—

A and if a **man shall come** among you **and say** this, (13:27)

Helaman 14:2–8—
There Will Be Great Signs in Heaven

And behold, he said unto them: Behold, I give unto you a sign; for five years more cometh,

   A and behold, then cometh the Son of God to redeem all those who shall **believe on his name**. (14:2)

      B And behold, this will I give unto you for **a sign** at the time of his coming;

         C for behold, there shall be **great lights in heaven**,

            D insomuch that in the night before he cometh there shall be **no darkness**, insomuch that it shall appear unto man as if it was day. (14:3)

               E Therefore, there shall be **one day and a night and a day**, as if it were one day and there were no night; and this shall be unto you for a sign;

                  F for **ye shall know** of the rising of the sun and also of its setting;

                  F therefore **they shall know** of a surety

               E that there shall be **two days and a night**;

            D nevertheless the **night shall not be darkened**; and it shall be the night before he is born. (14:4) And behold, there shall a new star arise, such an one as ye never have beheld; and this also shall be a sign unto you. (14:5)

         C And behold this is not all, there shall be many signs and **wonders in heaven**. (14:6)

      B And it shall come to pass that **ye shall all be amazed, and wonder**, insomuch ye shall fall to the earth. (14:7)

A And it shall come to pass that whosoever shall **believe on the Son of God**, the same shall have everlasting life. (14:8)

Helaman 14:15–17—
Resurrection versus Spiritual Death

A that thereby men may be brought into the **presence of the Lord**. (14:15)

    B Yea, behold, this death bringeth to pass the **resurrection**, and **redeemeth**

        C all mankind from the first **death**—

            D that **spiritual death**;

                E for all **mankind**,

                E by the fall of **Adam**

            D being **cut off from the presence** of the Lord,

        C are considered as **dead**, both as to things temporal and to things spiritual. (14:16)

    B But behold, the **resurrection** of Christ **redeemeth** mankind, yea, even all mankind,

A and bringeth them back into the **presence of the Lord**. (14:17)

Helaman 14:21–22—
Concerning Solid and Broken Rocks

A and the rocks which are upon the **face of this earth**, are **both above the earth and beneath**,

    B which ye know at this time are **solid**,

        C or the more part of it is one **solid mass**,

            D shall be **broken up**; (14:21)

            D Yea, they shall be **rent in twain**,

        C and shall ever after be found in **seams and in cracks**,

    B and in **broken** fragments

A upon the **face of the whole earth**, yea, **both above the earth and beneath**. (14:22)

Helaman 14:23 —
Concerning Mountains and Valleys

And behold, there shall be great tempests,
  A and there shall be many **mountains** laid low,
    B like unto a **valley**,
    B and there shall be many places which are now called **valleys**
  A which shall become **mountains**, whose height is great. (14:23)

Helaman 15:3 —
God Chastens Those He Loves

  A yea, the people of Nephi hath **he loved**,
    B and also hath **he chastened them**;
    B yea, in the days of their iniquities hath **he chastened them**
  A because **he loveth** them. (15:3)

Helaman 15:10–11 —
The Lord Prolongs Days of the Wicked

  A behold, the Lord shall bless them and **prolong their days**,
    B notwithstanding their **iniquity**— (15:10)
    B Yea, even if they should dwindle in **unbelief**
  A the Lord shall **prolong their days**, (15:11)

Helaman 16:1–3 —
Some Are Baptized;
Others Cast Stones at Samuel

And now, it came to pass that there were many who heard the words of Samuel, the Lamanite . . .
  A desiring that they might **be baptized** unto the Lord. (16:1)
    B But as many as there were who **did not believe in the words** of Samuel were angry with him;
      C and they cast **stones** at him upon the wall, and also many shot **arrows** at him as he stood upon the wall;
        D but the **Spirit of the Lord was with him**,

    C insomuch that they could not hit him with their **stones** neither with their **arrows**. (16:2)

   B Now when they saw that they could not hit him, there were many more who **did believe on his words**,

A insomuch that they went away unto Nephi to **be baptized**. (16:3)

3 Nephi

3 NEPHI 1:15—
NO DARKNESS AT NIGHT

A for behold, at the **going down of the sun**
  B here was **no darkness**;
    C and the **people began to be astonished**
  B because there was **no darkness**
A when the **night came**. (1:15)

3 NEPHI 2:7–8—
SIGN OF THE COMING OF CHRIST

A And **nine years** had passed away
  B from the time when the **sign was given**, which was spoken of by
the prophets, that **Christ should come** into the world. (2:7)
    C Now the Nephites began to **reckon their time** from this period
  B when the **sign was given**, or from the **coming of Christ**;
A therefore, **nine years** had passed away. (2:8)

3 NEPHI 2:14–16—
SOME LAMANITES UNITE WITH THE NEPHITES

A And it came to pass that those Lamanites who had united with the
Nephites
  B were **numbered among the Nephites**; (2:14)

C And their curse was taken from them, and their **skin became white** like unto the Nephites; (2:15)
　　C And their young men and their daughters **became exceedingly fair**,
　B and they were **numbered among the Nephites**,
A and were called **Nephites**. (2:16)

3 NEPHI 4:15—
ROBBERS DID NOT BATTLE

And it came to pass that the armies of the Nephites did return again to their place of security.
　A And it came to pass that this **nineteenth year** did pass away,
　　B and the robbers did not **come again** to battle;
　　B neither did they **come again**
　A in the **twentieth year**. (4:15)

3 NEPHI 4:24–25—
GIDGIDDONI COMMANDS HIS ARMIES

A therefore [Gidgiddoni] did send out his armies **in the night-time**,
　B and did cut off the **way of their retreat**,
　B and did place his armies in the **way of their retreat**. (4:25)
A And this did they do **in the night-time**, (4:26)

3 NEPHI 5:8—
MANY GREAT THINGS CAME TO PASS

A And there had **many things transpired** which, in the eyes of some, would be great and marvelous;
　B nevertheless, they **cannot all be written**
　　C in **this book**;
　　C yea, **this book**
　B **cannot contain** even a hundredth part
A of **what was done** among so many people in the space of twenty and five years; (5:8)

3 NEPHI 5:24–26—
THE LORD MADE A COVENANT WITH THE HOUSE OF JACOB

A And as surely **as the Lord liveth,**

    B will he **gather** in from the **four quarters of the earth** all the remnant of the seed of Jacob, who are scattered abroad upon all the face of the earth. (5:24)

        C And as he hath covenanted with **all the house of Jacob,**

            D even so shall the **covenant** wherewith he hath **covenanted**

                E with the **house of Jacob** be fulfilled in his own due time,

                E unto the restoring all the **house of Jacob** unto the knowledge

            D of the **covenant** that he hath **covenanted** with them. (5:25)

        C And then shall **they** know their Redeemer, who is Jesus Christ, the Son of God;

    B and then shall they be **gathered** in from the **four quarters of the earth** unto their own lands, from whence they have been dispersed;

A yea, **as the Lord liveth** so shall it be. Amen. (5:26)

3 NEPHI 6:13—
SOME ARE HUMBLE AND PENITENT

Some were lifted up in pride,

    A and others were exceedingly **humble;**

        B some **did return railing for railing,**

            C while others would receive **railing and persecution**

            C and all manner of **afflictions,**

        B and **would not turn and revile again,**

    A but were **humble** and penitent before God. (6:13)

3 NEPHI 6:18—
WILLFUL REBELLION VERSUS SINNING IN IGNORANCE

A Now they **did not sin ignorantly,**

    B for **they knew the will of God** concerning them,

    B for **it had been taught unto them;**

A therefore they **did wilfully rebel** against God. (6:18)

3 Nephi 6:20—
Some Individuals Testify Boldly

And there began to be men inspired from heaven and sent forth, standing among the people in all the land,

    A preaching and **testifying boldly** of the sins and iniquities of the people,

        B and testifying unto them concerning the **redemption**

            C which the **Lord would make** for his people,

        B or in other words, the **resurrection** of Christ;

    A and they did **testify boldly** of his death and sufferings. (6:20)

3 Nephi 7:2–4—
Tribes and Tribal Leaders

And the people were divided one against another;

    A and they did separate one from another into **tribes**,

        B every man according to his **family** and his **kindred** and **friends**; and thus they did destroy the government of the land. (7:2)

            C And every **tribe** did appoint a chief or a **leader** over them;

            C and thus they became **tribes** and **leaders** of tribes. (7:3)

        B Now behold, there was no man among them save he had much **family** and many **kindreds** and **friends**;

    A therefore their **tribes** became exceedingly great. (7:4)

3 Nephi 8:10—
Fate of the City of Moronihah

    A And the **earth** was carried up

        B upon the **city** of Moronihah

        B that in the place of the **city**

    A there became a great **mountain**. (8:10)

3 Nephi 8:16—
A Whirlwind Carries People Away

A And there were some who were **carried away** in the whirlwind;
  B and whither they went **no man knoweth**,
  B save **they know**
A that they were **carried away**. (8:16)

3 Nephi 9:16–17—
Those Who Receive Jesus Christ

A And the **scriptures** concerning my coming **are fulfilled**. (9:16)
  B And **as many** as have **received me**,
    C to them **have I given** to become the sons of God;
    C and even so **will I** to
  B **as many** as shall **believe on my name**,
A for behold, by me redemption cometh, and in me is the **law of Moses fulfilled**. (9:17)

3 Nephi 9:19—
Sacrificial Offerings Will Be Done Away

A And ye shall **offer up** unto me **no more**
  B the **shedding of blood**;
  B yea, your **sacrifices**
A and your burnt **offerings shall be done away**, (9:19)

3 Nephi 10:4–5—
Jesus Gathers Israel as a Hen Gathers Chickens

A O ye people of these great cities **which have fallen**,
  B who are descendants of Jacob, yea, who are of the **house of Israel**,
    C how oft have **I gathered you as a hen** gathereth her chickens under her wings,
      D and **have nourished you**. (10:4)
    C And again, how oft would **I have gathered you as a hen** gathereth her chickens under her wings,

B yea, O ye people of the **house of Israel**,
A **who have fallen**; (10:5)

3 NEPHI 10:12 —
THE RIGHTEOUS WERE SPARED

A And it was the more righteous part of the people **who were saved**,
    B and it was they who received the prophets and **stoned them not**;
    B and it was they who had **not shed the blood** of the saints,
A **who were spared**— (10:12)

3 NEPHI 11:29 —
THE DEVIL IS THE FATHER OF CONTENTION

For verily, verily I say unto you,
    A he that hath the **spirit of contention** is not of me,
        B but is of the **devil**,
        B who is the **father of contention**,
    A and he stirreth up the hearts of men **to contend with anger**, one
with another. (11:29)

3 NEPHI 15:5-9 —
THE LAW IS FULFILLED IN CHRIST

A Behold, **I am** he that gave **the law**, and I am he who covenanted with
my people Israel;
    B therefore, the **law** in me is fulfilled, for I have come to fulfil the
law; therefore it **hath an end**. (15:5)
        C Behold, **I do not destroy** the prophets,
            D for as many as have **not been fulfilled** in me,
            D verily I say unto you, **shall all be fulfilled**. (15:6)
        C And because I said unto you that old things have passed away, **I
do not destroy** that which hath been spoken concerning things
which are to come. (15:7)

B For behold, the covenant which I have made with my people is not all fulfilled; but the **law** which was given unto Moses **hath an end** in me. (15:8)

A Behold, **I am the law**, and the light. (15:9)

3 NEPHI 15:17–21— JESUS CHRIST HAS OTHER SHEEP

A a That **other sheep** I have
　b which are not of this **fold**;
　　c them also **I must bring**,
　　c and **they** shall **hear my voice**;
　b and there shall be one **fold**,
a and one **shepherd**. (15:17)
　B And now, **because of stiffneckedness and unbelief** they understood not my word;
　　C therefore I was commanded to say no more of the **Father** concerning this thing unto them. (15:18)
　　　D But, verily, I say unto you that the Father hath commanded me, and I tell it unto you, that ye were separated from among them **because of their iniquity**;
　　　D therefore it is **because of their iniquity** that they know not of you. (15:19)
　　C And verily, I say unto you again that the other tribes hath the **Father** separated from them; (15:20)
　B and it is **because of their iniquity** that they know not of them.
　And verily I say unto you, that ye are they of whom I said:
A a Other sheep I have
　b which are not of this **fold**;
　　c them also **I must bring**,
　　c and **they** shall **hear my voice**;
　b and there shall be one **fold**,
A a and one **shepherd**. (15:21)

3 Nephi 16:20—
Nations Will See God's Salvation

A The **Lord hath made bare his holy arm**
    B in the **eye of all the nations**;
    B and all the ends of the **earth shall see**
A the **salvation of God**.

3 Nephi 17:6–7—
Jesus Heals the Sick and the Afflicted

A Behold, my **bowels are filled**
    B with **compassion** towards you.
        C Have ye any that are **sick** among you? **Bring them hither**.
            D Have ye any that are **lame, or blind, or halt, or maimed**,
            D **or leprous, or** that are **withered, or** that are **deaf, or** that
            are **afflicted** in any manner?
        C **Bring them hither** and I will heal them,
    B for I have **compassion** upon you;
A my **bowels are filled** with mercy.

3 Nephi 17:12–13—
Jesus and the Multitude

A So they brought their little children and set them down **upon the
ground** round about him,
    B and **Jesus stood** in the midst;
        C and the multitude gave way till **they had all been brought**
        unto him. (17:12)
        C And it came to pass that when **they had all been brought**,
    B and **Jesus stood** in the midst,
A he commanded the multitude that they should kneel down **upon the
ground**. (17:13)

3 Nephi 17:24—
Angels Descend from Heaven
and Encircle Little Children

A and they saw **angels** descending out of heaven
  B as it were in the midst of **fire**;
    C and they came down and **encircled** those little ones about,
    C and they were **encircled**
  B about with **fire**;
A and the **angels** did minister unto them. (17:24)

3 Nephi 18:22—
Do Not Forbid People from Meeting with Saints

And behold, ye shall meet together oft;
  A and ye shall not **forbid** any man
    B from **coming unto you** when ye shall meet together,
    B but suffer them that they may **come unto you**
  A and **forbid** them not; (18:22)

3 Nephi 18:27–35—
"Numbered with My People"

A Behold verily, verily, I say unto you, I give unto you another commandment, and then I must **go unto my Father** that I may fulfil other commandments which he hath given me. (18:27)
  B And now behold, **this is the commandment which I give** unto you,
    C a that **ye shall not suffer**
      b any one knowingly to partake of **my flesh and blood**
        c **unworthily**, when ye shall minister it; (18:28)
          d For whoso **eateth and drinketh** my flesh and blood unworthily
          d **eateth and drinketh** damnation to his soul;
        c therefore if ye know that a man is **unworthy**
      b to eat and drink of **my flesh and blood**
    a ye shall **forbid** him. (18:29)

D Nevertheless, **ye shall not cast him out** from among you, but ye shall **minister** unto him and shall pray for him unto the Father, in my name; and if it so be that **he repenteth** and is baptized in my name, then shall ye receive him, and shall minister unto him of my flesh and blood. (18:30)

    E But if **he repent not** he shall not be numbered among my people, that he may not destroy my people, for behold I know my sheep, and they are numbered. (18:31)

D Nevertheless, **ye shall not cast him out** of your synagogues, or your places of worship, for unto such shall ye continue to **minister**; for ye know not but what they will **return and repent**, and come unto me with full purpose of heart, and I shall heal them;

C and **ye shall be the means** of bringing **salvation** unto them. (18:32) Therefore, keep these sayings which I have commanded you that ye come not under condemnation; for wo unto him whom the Father condemneth. (18:33)

B And **I give you these commandments** because of the disputations which have been among you. And blessed are ye if ye have no disputations among you. (18:34)

A And now **I go unto the Father**, because it is expedient that I should go unto the Father for your sakes. (18:35)

3 NEPHI 19:2–3—
WORD TRAVELS REGARDING JESUS' MINISTERING

A And it was **noised abroad** among the people immediately,

  B before it was yet **dark**,

    C that the multitude had **seen Jesus**,

      D and that **he had ministered unto them**,

    C and that he would also **show himself** on the morrow unto the multitude. (19:2)

  B Yea, and even all the **night**

A it was **noised abroad** concerning Jesus; (19:3)

3 Nephi 23:3—
Isaiah's Words Will Be Fulfilled

A And all **things that he spake**
 B **have been**
 B and **shall be**,
A even according to the **words which he spake**. (23:3)

3 Nephi 26:16–18—
Babes Utter Marvelous Things

A yea, even babes did open their mouths and utter **marvelous things**; and the things which they did utter were **forbidden** that there should not **any man write them**. (26:16)
 B And it came to pass that the disciples whom **Jesus** had chosen
  C began from that time forth to **baptize** and to teach as many as did come unto them;
  C and as many as were **baptized**
 B in the name of **Jesus** were filled with the Holy Ghost. (26:17)
A And many of them saw and heard **unspeakable things**, which are **not lawful to be written**. (26:18)

3 Nephi 27:7–9—
Pray to the Father in Jesus Christ's Name

A Therefore, **whatsoever** ye shall do, ye shall do it **in my name**; therefore ye shall call the church in my name; and ye shall **call upon the Father in my name** that he will bless the church for my sake. (27:7)
 B And how be it **my church** save it be called in **my name**?
  C For if a church be called in **Moses' name** then it be **Moses' church**;
  C or if it be called in the **name of a man** then it be the **church of a man**;
 B but if it be called in **my name** then it is **my church**, if it so be that they (27:8) are built upon my gospel. Verily I say unto you, that ye are built upon my gospel;

A therefore ye shall call **whatsoever** things ye do call, **in my name**;
therefore if ye **call upon the Father**, for the church, if it be **in my name**
the Father will hear you; (27:9)

3 NEPHI 27:13—
JESUS' GOSPEL

A Behold I have **given unto you**
  B my **gospel**,
  B and this is the **gospel**
A which I have **given unto you**— (27:13)

3 NEPHI 28:1–4—
JESUS GRANTS THE DESIRE OF THE TWELVE DISCIPLES

A a And it came to pass when **Jesus had said** these words,
  b he spake unto **his disciples**, one by one,
    c saying unto them:
      d What is it that **ye desire of me**,
        e after that **I am gone** to the Father? (28:1)
B a And **they all spake**, save it were three, saying:
  b We desire that after we have lived unto the **age of man**, that our
ministry, wherein thou hast called us, may have an end,
    c that we may speedily **come unto thee** in thy kingdom. (28:2)
B a And **he said** unto them: Blessed are ye because ye desired this
thing of me;
    b therefore, after that ye are **seventy and two years old**
      c ye shall **come unto me** in my kingdom; and with me ye shall
find rest. (28:3)
A a And when **he had spoken** unto them,
  b he turned himself unto **the three**,
    c and **said unto them**:
      d What will ye that **I should do** unto you,
        e when **I am gone** unto the Father? (28:4)

3 Nephi 28:13–14—
The Three Nephites See Unspeakable Things

And behold, the heavens were opened, and they were caught up into heaven,
- **A** and **saw and heard** unspeakable things. (28:13)
  - **B** And it was forbidden them that **they should utter**;
  - **B** neither was it given unto them power that **they could utter**
- **A** the things which they **saw and heard**; (28:14)

3 Nephi 28:37–38—
The Three Nephites' Bodies Are Changed

But behold, since I wrote, I have inquired of the Lord, and he hath made it manifest unto me
- **A** that there must needs be a **change wrought** upon their bodies,
  - **B** or else it needs be that they must **taste of death**; (28:37)
  - **B** Therefore, that they might not **taste of death**
- **A** there was a **change wrought** upon their bodies, (28:38)

4 Nephi and Mormon

4 NEPHI 1:31–34—
PERSECUTIONS AGAINST THE
THREE TRANSLATED DISCIPLES

Nevertheless, and notwithstanding all these miracles,
> A the people did **harden their hearts**, and did seek **to kill** them, even
> as the Jews at Jerusalem sought to kill Jesus, according to his word. (1:31)
>> B And they did **cast them** into furnaces of fire, and they **came forth
>> receiving no harm**. (1:32)
>> B And they also **cast them** into dens of wild beasts, and they did
>> play with the wild beasts even as a child with a lamb; and they did
>> **come forth** from among them, **receiving no harm**. (1:33)
> A Nevertheless, the people did **harden their hearts**, for they were led
> by many priests and false prophets to build up many churches, and to
> **do all manner of iniquity**. (1:34)

4 NEPHI 1:34—
WICKED PEOPLE SMITE JESUS' DISCIPLES

> A And they did **smite**
>> B upon the **people of Jesus**;
>> B but the **people of Jesus**
> A did not **smite** again. (1:34)

MORMON 1:16—
MORMON IS FORBIDDEN TO PREACH

A And I did endeavor to **preach** unto this people,
   B but my **mouth was shut**,
   B and **I was forbidden**
A that I should **preach** unto them; (1:16)

MORMON 2:8—
CARNAGE THROUGHOUT THE LAND

A therefore there was **blood and carnage** spread throughout all the **face of the land**,
   B both on the **part of the Nephites**
   B and also on the **part of the Lamanites**;
A and it was one complete **revolution** throughout all the **face of the land**. (2:8)

MORMON 9:15—
GOD IS A GOD OF MIRACLES

A And now, O all ye that have imagined up unto yourselves a **god who can do no miracles**,
   B I would ask of you, **have all these things passed**, of which I have spoken?
   B Has the end come yet? Behold I say unto you, Nay;
A and God has not ceased to be a **God of miracles**. (9:15)

MORMON 9:18—
JESUS CHRIST AND HIS APOSTLES DO MIGHTY MIRACLES

A And who shall say that **Jesus Christ**
   B did not many **mighty miracles**?
   B And there were many **mighty miracles**
A wrought by the hands of the **apostles**. (9:18)

MORMON 9:19 —
GOD IS A GOD OF MIRACLES

A And if there were **miracles** wrought then,

   B why has God **ceased to be a God** of miracles

      C and yet be an **unchangeable Being**?

      C And behold, I say unto you **he changeth not**;

   B if so he would **cease to be God**; and he ceaseth not to be God,

A and is a God of **miracles**. (9:19)

Ether

ETHER 1:5 —
MORONI GIVES A PARTIAL ACCOUNT OF THE JAREDITES

A But behold, I **give** not
   B the **full account**,
   B but a **part of the account**
A I **give**, (1:5)

ETHER 1:35 —
JARED'S LANGUAGE IS NOT CONFOUNDED

[T]he brother of Jared did cry unto the Lord, and the Lord had compassion upon Jared;
   A therefore he did **not confound**
      B the language of **Jared**;
      B and **Jared** and his brother
   A were **not confounded**.

ETHER 1:38 —
JARED'S BROTHER PRAYS

And it came to pass that Jared spake again unto his brother, saying:
   A Go and **inquire of the Lord**
      B whether he will **drive us out** of the land,
      B and if he will **drive us out** of the land,
   A **cry unto him** whither we shall go. (1:38)

ETHER 3:4-5—
THE LORD HAS ALL POWER

A And I know, O Lord, that thou hast **all power**,
   B and **can do** whatsoever thou wilt for the benefit of man;
     C therefore touch these stones, O Lord, with thy finger, and prepare them that they may **shine forth** in darkness;
     C and they shall **shine forth** unto us in the vessels which we have prepared, that we may have light while we shall cross the sea. (3:4)
   B Behold, O Lord, thou **canst do** this.
A We know that thou art able to show forth **great power**, (3:5)

ETHER 3:19-20—
THE BROTHER OF JARED SEES JESUS' FINGER

A And because of the **knowledge** of this man he could not be kept from beholding **within the veil**;
   B and he saw the **finger of Jesus**, which, when he saw, he fell with fear; for **he knew**
   B that it was the **finger of the Lord**; and he had faith no longer, for **he knew**, nothing doubting. (3:19)
A Wherefore, having this perfect **knowledge** of God, he could not be kept from **within the veil**; (3:20)

ETHER 6:9—
JARED'S BROTHER SINGS PRAISES TO THE LORD

And they did sing praises unto the Lord; yea, the brother of Jared did sing praises unto the Lord,
   A and he did thank and **praise the Lord**
     B all the **day** long;
     B and when the **night** came,
   A they did not cease to **praise the Lord**. (6:9)

ETHER 6:14–20—
JARED'S FAMILY AND FRIENDS

A And **Jared had four sons**; and they were called Jacom, and Gilgah, and Mahah, and Orihah. (6:14)

    B And the **brother of Jared**

        C also begat **sons and daughters**. (6:15)

            D And the **friends of Jared and his brother were in number** about twenty and two souls; and they also begat sons and daughters before they came to the promised land;

                E and therefore they began **to be many**. (6:16)

                    F And **they were taught** to walk humbly before the Lord;

                    F and **they were also taught** from on high. (6:17)

                E And it came to pass that they began to spread upon the face of the land, and **to multiply** and to till the earth; and they did wax strong in the land. (6:18)

            D And the brother of Jared began to be old, and saw that he must soon go down to the grave; wherefore he said unto Jared: Let us gather together our **people that we may number them**, that we may know of them what they will desire of us before we go down to our graves. (6:19) And accordingly the people were gathered together.

        C Now the number of the **sons and the daughters**

    B of the **brother of Jared** were twenty and two souls;

A and the number of sons and daughters of Jared were twelve, **he having four sons**. (6:20)

ETHER 10:23—
WORKING WITH VARIOUS METALS

A And **they did work** in all manner of ore,

    B and they did make **gold**, and **silver**, and **iron**, and **brass**, and all manner of metals;

        C and they did **dig it out** of the earth;

        C wherefore they did **cast up** mighty heaps of earth to get ore,

    B of **gold**, and of **silver**, and of **iron**, and of **copper**.

A And **they did work** all manner of fine work. (10:23)

ETHER 12:7—
CHRIST SHOWS HIMSELF BY FAITH

A For it was by **faith**
  B that **Christ showed himself** unto our fathers,
    C after **he had risen** from the dead;
  B and **he showed not himself** unto them
A until after they had **faith** in him; (12:7)

ETHER 12:17—
THE THREE NEPHITES HAVE FAITH

A And it was by **faith** that the three disciples
  B obtained a **promise**
    C that they should **not taste of death**;
  B and they obtained not the **promise**
A until after their **faith**. (12:17)

ETHER 12:23–25—
THE LORD "MADE US MIGHTY IN WORD"

A And I said unto him: Lord, the **Gentiles will mock** at these things,
  B because of our **weakness in writing**;
    C for Lord **thou hast made us mighty in word** by faith,
      D but **thou hast not made us mighty in writing**;
        E for thou hast made all **this people that they could speak much**, because of the Holy Ghost which thou hast given them; (12:23)
        E And thou hast made us that **we could write but little**, because of the awkwardness of our hands.
      D Behold, **thou hast not made us mighty in writing** like unto the brother of Jared, for thou madest him that the things which he wrote were mighty even as thou art, unto the overpowering of man to read them. (12:24)
    C **Thou hast also made our words powerful** and great, even that we cannot write them;

B wherefore, when **we write we behold our weakness**, and stumble because of the placing of our words;

A and I fear lest the **Gentiles shall mock** at our words. (12:25)

ETHER 12:32—
WE MUST HAVE HOPE

And I also remember that thou hast said

    A that **thou hast prepared a house** for man, yea, even among the mansions of thy Father,

      B in which **man might have** a more excellent **hope**;

      B wherefore **man must hope**,

    A or he cannot receive an inheritance in the **place which thou hast prepared**. (12:32)

ETHER 13:4–6—
BUILDING A NEW JERUSALEM

Behold, Ether saw the days of Christ,

    A and he spake concerning a **New Jerusalem upon this land**. (13:4)

      B And he spake also concerning the **house of Israel**, and the Jerusalem from whence Lehi should come—

         C after it should be destroyed it should be **built up again**, a **holy city** unto the Lord;

            D wherefore, it could **not be a new Jerusalem**

            D for **it had been in a time of old**;

         C but it should be **built up again**, and become a **holy city** of the Lord;

      B and it should be built unto the **house of Israel**. (13:5)

    A And that a **New Jerusalem** should be built **upon this land**, (13:6)

ETHER 13:12—
THE FIRST AND THE LAST

And when these things come, bringeth to pass the scripture which saith,

  A there are they who were **first**,

    B who shall be **last**;

    B and there are they who were **last**,

  A who shall be **first**. (13:12)

Moroni

MORONI 1:2-3—
PUTTING TO DEATH THOSE WHO DO NOT DENY CHRIST

For behold, their wars are exceedingly fierce among themselves;
    A and because of their hatred they **put to death** every Nephite
        B that will not **deny the Christ**. (1:2)
        B And I, Moroni, will not **deny the Christ**;
    A wherefore, I wander whithersoever I can for the **safety of mine own life**. (1:3)

MORONI 1:4—
MORONI WRITES MORE THINGS

A Wherefore, **I write a few more things**,
    B contrary to that which **I had supposed**;
    B for **I had supposed** not to have written any more;
A but **I write a few more things**, (1:4)

MORONI 2:1-3—
CHRIST GIVES HIS TWELVE DISCIPLES POWER

A The **words of Christ, which he spake** unto his **disciples**, the twelve whom he had chosen, as he **laid his hands** upon them— (2:1)
    B And he called them by name, saying: Ye shall call on the Father in **my name**, in mighty prayer; and after ye have done this

    C ye shall have **power** that to him upon whom ye shall lay your hands,
    C ye shall give the **Holy Ghost**;
  B and in **my name** shall ye give it, for thus do mine apostles. (2:2)
A Now **Christ spake these words** unto them at the time of his first appearing; and the multitude heard it not, but the **disciples** heard it; and on as many as they **laid their hands**, fell the Holy Ghost. (2:3)

MORONI 7:11—
A GOOD FOUNTAIN VERSUS A BITTER FOUNTAIN

A For behold, a **bitter** fountain
  B cannot bring forth **good** water;
  B neither can a **good** fountain
A bring forth **bitter** water; (7:11)

MORONI 7:11—
THE DEVIL'S SERVANT CANNOT FOLLOW CHRIST

A wherefore, a man being a **servant of the devil**
  B cannot **follow Christ**;
  B and if he **follow Christ**
A he cannot be a **servant of the devil**. (7:11)

MORONI 7:14—
EVIL IS NOT OF GOD

Wherefore, take heed, my beloved brethren,
  A that ye do not judge that which is **evil**
    B to be of **God**,
    B or that which is good and of **God**
  A to be of the **devil**. (7:14)

MORONI 7:27–29—
MIRACLES HAVE NOT CEASED

A Wherefore, my beloved **brethren, have miracles ceased**

  B because **Christ hath ascended into heaven**, and hath sat down on the right hand of God,

    C to claim of the Father his rights of mercy which he hath upon the **children of men**? (7:27)

      D For he hath answered the ends of the law, and he claimeth all those **who have faith in him**;

      D and they **who have faith in him** will cleave unto every good thing;

    C wherefore he advocateth the cause of the **children of men**;

  B and **he dwelleth eternally in the heavens**. (7:28)

A And because he hath done this, my beloved **brethren, have miracles ceased**? (7:29)

MORONI 9:22—
RETURN TO GOD, OR PERISH

I pray unto God that he will spare thy life,

  A to witness the **return** of his people **unto him**,

    B or their utter **destruction**;

    B for I know that they must **perish**

  A except they repent and **return unto him**. (9:22)

MORONI 10:4–5—
CHRIST MANIFESTS TRUTH

A [Christ] will manifest the **truth** of it unto you,

  B by the **power of the Holy Ghost**. (10:4)

  B And by the **power of the Holy Ghost**

A ye may know the **truth** of all things. (10:5)

Appendix

LIST OF CHIASMS IN THE BOOK OF ISAIAH

The following list presents about one hundred and thirty examples of chiasmus in Isaiah. Note that many chiastic structures in the Hebrew language are not always evident when translated into English. This is partly due to the different sentence structures in the two languages. Many of the following examples of chiasmus are followed with the word *Hebrew* in parentheses, indicating that the chiasmus exists in the Hebrew but has lost its chiastic value in the English translation.

Isa. 1:11 I have eaten/rams, fatted steers/ /bulls, lambs, male goats/I do not desire

Isa. 1:21 prostitute/justice/ /righteousness/murderers

Isa. 1:21–26 faithful town/justice . . . righteousness/silver . . . dross/rulers . . . thieves/the LORD of Hosts/ /the mighty One of Israel/adversaries . . . enemies/dross . . . slag/judges . . . counselors/faithful town

Isa. 2:3 from Zion/law/ /word of the LORD/from Jerusalem

Isa. 2:3–5 House of the God of Jacob . . . we may walk/nations/swords into plowshares/ /spears into pruninghooks/nation . . . nation/house of Jacob . . . let us walk

Isa. 3:1–8 Jerusalem . . . Judah/bread/judge . . . prophet . . . captain/ young people/ /everyone by another/ /every one by a neighbor/young person/you will be our leader/bread/Jerusalem . . . Judah

Isa. 3:8 has stumbled/Jerusalem/ /Judah/has fallen (Hebrew)

Isa. 5:7 vineyard/house of Israel/ /men of Judah/delightful plant

Isa. 5:11–13 strong drink . . . wine/banquets/deeds of the LORD/ /work of His hands/ hungry/thirst

Isa. 5:14-17 opened its mouth/bow down . . . humbled/exalted/ /shows himself holy/feed . . . feed

Isa. 5:20 evil/good/ /good/evil

Isa. 5:20 darkness/light/ /light/darkness

Isa. 5:20 bitter/sweet/ /sweet/bitter

Isa. 5:21 wise/in their own eyes/ /in their own sight/understanding

Isa. 6:7 is removed/your iniquity/ /your sin/atoned

Isa. 6:10 heart/ears/eyes/ /eyes/ears/hearts

Isa. 7:7-9 it will not happen/head . . . head/Ephraim will be shattered/ /it is no longer a people/head . . . head/will not hold firm

Isa. 7:11-12 LORD/Ahaz/ask/ /ask/Ahaz/LORD

Isa. 7:22 eat/butter/ /butter/eat

Isa. 9:21 Manasseh/Ephraim/ /Ephraim/Manasseh

Isa. 10:4 to crouch/under the prisoners/ /under the slain/to fall (Hebrew)

Isa. 10:6 I will send him/against a godless nation/ /against the people of my wrath/will I command him

Isa. 10:20-21 remnant of Israel/survivors of the house of Jacob/rely upon him who smote them/ /rely upon the LORD/remnant will return/remnant of Jacob

Isa. 10:24 Assyria/smite you with a rod/ /lift up his staff/Egypt

Isa. 11:1 will come forth/rod/ /branch/will grow (Hebrew)

Isa. 11:4 smite the earth/rod of his mouth/ /breath of his lips/slay the wicked

Isa. 11:6 will dwell/wolf . . . with the lamb/ /leopard . . . with the kid/will lie down (Hebrew)

Isa. 11:8 will play/nursing babe . . . on the hole of the viper/ /toddler . . . on the hole of the viper/ will put his hand (Hebrew)

Isa. 11:13 Ephraim/Judah/ /Judah/Ephraim

Isa. 13:10 will be darkened/sun/ /moon/will not cause its light to shine (Hebrew)

Isa. 13:16 plundered/their houses/ /their wives/ravished

Isa. 13:21 will dwell there/owls/ /wild goats/will leap about there (Hebrew)

Isa. 14:15 Sheol/brought down/ /to the depths/pit

Isa. 14:25 be removed/his yoke/ /his burden/be removed (Hebrew)

Isa. 14:25 to break the Assyrian/My land/ /My mountains/I will trample him

Isa. 14:30 shall feed/poor/ /needy/lie down in safety (Hebrew)

Isa. 14:30 I will kill/your root/ /your remnant/it shall slay

Isa. 16:7-12 Moab/Kir-hareseth/Heshbon/Sibmah/Jazer/ /Jazer/Sibmah/ Heshbon/Kir-hareseth/Moab

Isa. 17:10 you have forgotten/*God of Your Salvation/* /*Rock of Your Stronghold*/you have not remembered

Isa. 18:6 will summer upon them/birds of prey/ /wild animals/will winter upon them (Hebrew)

Isa. 19:21 LORD/be known/Egyptians/ /Egyptians/know/LORD

Isa. 21:12 you/enquire/ /enquire/you

Isa. 22:19 I will thrust you/from your station/ /from your position/he will cast you

Isa. 22:22 open/shut/ /shut/open

Isa. 25:10–11 hand of the LORD/trodden down/ /trodden down/his hands

Isa. 26:7 righteous/level/ /level/righteous

Isa. 26:9–10 righteousness/learn/inhabitants of the world/ /wicked/learn/righteousness (Hebrew)

Isa. 26:19 will live/dead men/ /bodies/will . . . arise (Hebrew)

Isa. 27:5 he will make/peace/ /peace/he will make (Hebrew)

Isa. 27:11 will not have compassion/their Maker/ /their Fashioner/will show them no favor (Hebrew)

Isa. 28:12 to those whom He has said/this is the rest/ /give rest to the weary/ /this is the resting place/they are not willing to hear

Isa. 28:15–18 covenant with death . . . Sheol, we made an agreement . . . overflowing scourge/lie our place of refuge . . . shelter/laying a stone/ precious cornerstone/ /sure foundation/measuring line . . . plumb line/ refuge of lies . . . shelter/covenant with death . . . agreement with Sheol . . . overflowing scourge

Isa. 29:10 shut your eyes/prophets/ /your rulers/ /seers/He has covered

Isa. 29:14 shall perish/wisdom of their wise/ /understanding of their prudent/will be hid (Hebrew)

Isa. 29:17 will be turned/Lebanon/fertile field/ /fertile field/forest/be regarded (Hebrew)

Isa. 30:8 write it/tablet/ /book/inscribe it (Hebrew)

Isa. 30:22 you will defile/idols, overlaid with silver/ /gold-plated molten images/you will cast them away (Hebrew)

Isa. 32:1 will reign/king/ /princes/will govern (Hebrew)

Isa. 32:3 will not be closed/eyes of those who see/ /ears of those who hear/will listen (Hebrew)

Isa. 32:6 folly/speaks/ /works/iniquity (Hebrew)

Isa. 32:6 to make empty/the hungry/ /the thirsty/to deprive (Hebrew)

Isa. 32:16 reside/ in the wilderness/justice/ /righteousness/in the fruitful field/will dwell (32:16)

Isa. 33:14 sinners in Zion/are afraid/ /trembling seizes/the godless

Isa. 33:17 King/your eyes will envision/ /they will see/land (Hebrew)

Isa. 34:4 host/heaven/ /heavens/host

Isa. 34:5–8 Edom/judgment/fat/lambs and goats/sacrifice/ /slaughter/ bulls . . . mighty ones/fat/vengeance/Zion

Isa. 35:1–2 be joyful/blossom/ /blossom/be joyful

Isa. 35:10 everlasting joy/upon their heads/ /they will obtain/exultation and rejoicing

Isa. 36:18–19 deliver . . . hand/where are the gods/ /where are the gods/delivered . . . hand

Isa. 38:12 My dwelling/is pulled up/ /is removed from me/like a tent of a shepherd

Isa. 40:12 measured/hollow of His hand/waters/ /heavens/width/ marked off (Hebrew)

Isa. 40:14 made Him understand/taught him/ /taught him/made Him know the way of understanding

Isa. 40:26 Lift up . . . on high/your eyes/ /see/who created these (Hebrew)

Isa. 40:26 calling them all by name/abundant might/ /mighty power/not one is missing

Isa. 40:27 is hidden/my way/from the LORD/ /my God/my judgment/is passed over (Hebrew)

Isa. 40:28–31 does not faint/is not weary/He gives power to the faint/ strength/youth/ /young men/strength/they will go up with wings like eagles/not grow weary/not faint

Isa. 41:4 I the LORD/first/ /last ones/I am He

Isa. 42:4 he have established/in the earth/justice/ /his law/the islands/ will wait (Hebrew)

Isa. 42:12 let them give glory/the LORD/ /his praise/declare

Isa. 42:15 lay waste/mountains and hills/ /all their vegetation/dry up (Hebrew)

Isa. 43:1–21 your Fashioner/waters . . . rivers/fire . . . scorched/LORD, God, Holy One, Savior/Egypt, Cush, Seba/I give, I will bring, gather, say, created, fashioned/you are My witnesses/I am the LORD/ /there is no Savior besides Me/ /you are My witnesses/I act/Babylon, Chaldeans/LORD, Holy One, Creator, King/snuffed like a wick/water . . . rivers/I have fashioned this people

Isa. 43:18 do not remember/former things/ /things of old/nor consider

Isa. 43:20–21 wilderness/desert/beast/ /jackals and ostriches/wilderness/ desert

Isa. 44:21 Israel/My servant/ /My servant/Israel

Isa. 45:1 before him/I will loose/ /to open/before him (Hebrew)

146

Isa. 45:22–25 ends of the earth/God/righteousness/every knee/ /every tongue/righteousness/Lord/seed of Israel

Isa. 48:1 are called/Israel/ /Judah/came forth

Isa. 48:1 who swear/by the name of the LORD/ /the God of Israel/ acknowledge

Isa. 48:3, 5 announced/the former things/ /of old/told

Isa. 48:4 iron/neck/ /forehead/brass (Hebrew)

Isa. 48:18 like a river/your peace/ /your righteousness/like the waves of the sea (Hebrew)

Isa. 48:21 waters/rock/ /rock/water

Isa. 49:1 O you house of Israel/all you that are broken off and are driven out/ /because of the wickedness of the pastors of My people/ /all you that are broken off, that are scattered abroad/O house of Israel

Isa. 49:1 LORD has called me/from the womb/ /from my mother's belly/ he assigned my name

Isa. 49:1–6 islands/peoples/womb/made me a sharpened arrow/You are my servant/ /I have labored/my reward is with my God/womb/tribes of Jacob/ends of the earth

Isa. 49:11 And I will make all My mountains/a way/ /and My highways/ will be exalted

Isa. 49:13 has comforted/His people/ /His afflicted/will have compassion (Hebrew)

Isa. 49:14 has forsaken me/LORD/ /Lord/has forgotten me (Hebrew)

Isa. 49:18 as with an ornament/you will surely clothe all of them/ /bind them on /as a bride (Hebrew)

Isa. 49:22 I will lift up/nations/ /peoples/raise up (Hebrew)

Isa. 49:22 they shall bring/sons in their lap/ /daughters . . . upon their shoulders/will be carried (Hebrew)

Isa. 49:24–25 prey/captives/ /captives/prey

Isa. 50:1 thus says the LORD/Have I put you away/have I cast you off forever/thus says the Lord

Isa. 50:1 your mother/put you away/sold/ /sold/put you away/your mother (Hebrew)

Isa. 50:3 clothe/blackness/ /sackcloth/covering

Isa. 50:4 he wakens/morning/ /morning/he wakens

Isa. 51:4 hearken/to me/My people/ /My nation/to me/give ear (Hebrew)

Isa. 51:7 fear not/insults of men/ /their revilings/neither be dismayed (Hebrew)

Isa. 51:11 will overtake them/gladness and joy/ /sorrow and sighing/will flee away

Isa. 51:15 I am the LORD your God/who stirs up the sea/ /and its waves roar/the LORD of Hosts is His name

Isa. 51:23 pass over/like the ground/ /like the street/passed over

Isa. 53:7 He opened not His mouth/as a lamb/ /as a ewe lamb/He openeth not his mouth

Isa. 54:2 enlarge/the place of your tent/ /the curtains of your habitations/stretched out (Hebrew)

Isa. 54:2 lengthen/your cords/ /your stakes/strengthen (Hebrew)

Isa. 54:13 your children/taught of the LORD/ /peace/your children

Isa. 55:8–9 My thoughts/your thoughts/your ways/My ways/heavens are higher/ /than the earth/My ways/your ways/My thoughts/your thoughts

Isa. 56:5 I will give/name/ /name/I will give (Hebrew)

Isa. 56:9 beasts of the field/ /come to eat/ /beasts in the forest

Isa. 57:15 contrite/lowly in spirit/ /lowly in spirit/contrite

Isa. 57:20–21 the wicked/tossing sea/it cannot be quiet/ /its waters toss up mire and dirt/no peace/the wicked

Isa. 58:10 pour out/your soul/ /afflicted/satisfy (Hebrew)

Isa. 59:3 have spoken/lies/ /wickedness/mutters (Hebrew)

Isa. 59:16–17 salvation/righteousness/ /righteousness/salvation

Isa. 60:1–3

A Arise,
  B shine;
    C for your light has come,
      D and the glory
        E of the LORD
          F has risen upon you.
            G For behold, the darkness will cover the earth,
            G and gross darkness the people:
          F will arise on you,
        E but the LORD
      D and His glory will appear on you.
    C And the nations will go to your light
  B and kings to the brightness
A of your rising. (Hebrew)

Isa. 60:13 to beautify/the place of My sanctuary/ /the place of My feet/make . . . glorious (Hebrew)

Isa. 60:16 you will suck/the milk of nations/ /the breast of kings/you will suck (Hebrew)

Isa. 62:1 as brightness/her righteousness/ /her salvation/as burning torch (Hebrew)

Isa. 63:16 You are our Father/Abraham does not know us/ /Israel does not acknowledge us/You, O LORD, are our Father

Isa. 65:18 be joyful forever/I create/ /I create/for joy . . . for exultation

Selected Bibliography

Parry, Donald W. *Harmonizing Isaiah: Combining Ancient Sources.* Provo, UT: Neal A. Maxwell Institute for Religious Scholarship, Brigham Young University, 2001.

———. *Poetic Parallelisms in the Book of Mormon: The Complete Text Reformatted.* Salt Lake City: Stonewell Press, 2018. First published as *The Book of Mormon Text Reformatted according to Parallelistic Structure.* Provo: FARMS, 1992; then updated and revised as *Poetic Parallelisms in the Book of Mormon.* Provo, UT: Neal A. Maxwell Institute for Religious Scholarship, Brigham Young University, 2007.

———. *Preserved in Translation: Hebrew and Other Ancient Literary Forms in the Book of Mormon.* Provo, UT: Religious Studies Center, 2020.

Welch, John W. "Chiasm, Chiasmus: I. Ancient Near East and Hebrew Bible/Old Testament." In *Encyclopedia of the Bible and Its Reception*, edited by Dale C. Allison et al., 5:78–79. 30 vols. Boston, MA: Walter de Gruyter, 2012.

———, ed. *Chiasmus in Antiquity: Structures, Analyses, Exegesis.* Hildesheim: Gerstenberg, 1918.

———. "Chiasmus in the Book of Mormon." In *Book of Mormon Authorship: New Light on Ancient Origins,* edited by Noel B. Reynolds, 33–52. Provo, UT: Religious Studies Center, 1982.

———. "Chiasmus in the Book of Mormon." *BYU Studies Quarterly* 10, no. 3 (1969): 69–83.

———. "Chiasmus in the Book of Mormon." *New Era*, Feb. 1972, 6–11.

———. "Criteria for Identifying and Evaluating the Presence of Chiasmus." *Journal of Book of Mormon Studies* 4, no. 2 (1995): 1–14.

———. "How Long Did It Take Joseph Smith to Translate the Book of Mormon?" *Ensign*, Jan. 1988, 46–47.

———. "A Masterpiece: Alma 36." In *Rediscovering the Book of Mormon*, edited by John L. Sorenson and Melvin J. Thorne, 114–131. Provo, UT: FARMS, 1991.

———. "What Does Chiasmus in the Book of Mormon Prove?" in Noel B. Reynolds, ed., 199–224. *Book of Mormon Authorship Revisited*. Provo, UT: FARMS, 1997.

Welch, John W., and Donald W. Parry, eds. *Chiasmus: The State of the Art. BYU Studies Quarterly* 59, no. 2 (2020): 107–127.